CENTURIES OF GREATNESS

CENTURIES OF GREATNESS

THE WEST AFRICAN KINGDOMS: 750-1900

Philip Koslow

CHELSEA HOUSE PUBLISHERS
New York   Philadelphia

FRONTISPIECE   This bronze mask was created in the kingdom of Benin, renowned for its magnificent wealth and brilliant aesthetic achievements.

ON THE COVER   Cast in bronze, these elaborately clothed court dignitaries once graced the royal palace in the kingdom of Benin.

Chelsea House Publishers
Editorial Director   Richard Rennert
Executive Managing Editor   Karyn Gullen Browne
Copy Chief   Robin James
Picture Editor   Adrian G. Allen
Art Director   Robert Mitchell
Manufacturing Director   Gerald Levine

Milestones in Black American History
Senior Editor   Marian W. Taylor
Series Originator and Adviser   Benjamin I. Cohen
Series Consultants   Clayborne Carson, Darlene Clark Hine
Series Designer   Rae Grant

Staff for CENTURIES OF GREATNESS
Assistant Editor   Margaret Dornfeld
Copy Editor   Catherine Iannone
Editorial Assistant   Annie McDonnell
Picture Researcher   Sandy Jones

First Printing

1   3   5   7   9   8   6   4   2

Library of Congress Cataloging-in-Publication Data

Koslow, Philip.
    Centuries of Greatness, 750–1900: the West African kingdoms/Philip Koslow.
        p. cm.—(Milestones in Black American history)
    Includes bibliographical references and index.
    ISBN 0-7910-2266-8.
    ISBN 0-7910-2692-2 (pbk.)
    1. Africa, West—History—To 1884—Juvenile literature. [1. Africa, West—History—To 1884.] I. Title. II. Series.
DT476.K67 1994   93-40667
966—dc20   CIP
                                                                                          AC

CONTENTS

MILESTONES IN BLACK AMERICAN HISTORY

INTRODUCTION

On a sunny morning in July 1796, Mungo Park, a Scottish explorer, achieved the goal of his long, difficult trek through West Africa and reached the banks of the Niger River. Along the river was a cluster of four large towns. The sight of these settlements, which together made up the city of Segu, dazzled Park as much as the spectacle of the broad, shining river. "The view of this extensive city," he wrote, "the numerous canoes upon the river; the crowded population; and the cultivated state of the surrounding country, found altogether a prospect of civilization and magnificence, which I little expected to find in the bosom of Africa."

Park's account of his journey, *Travels in the Interior Districts of Africa*, became a best-seller in England. But his positive reflections on Africa had little lasting effect on his readers. Later explorers, such as Richard Burton, who harped upon the "backwardness" of Africans, achieved far more attention and fame than did Park, who died during a second trip to Africa in 1805. By the end of the 18th century, European merchants were engaged in a profitable trade in slaves along the West African coast, and any real appreciation of the richness of African culture could only work against them. Nor did the European attitude change markedly in the decades that followed. Exactly 100 years after Park's arrival at Segu, a professor at England's Oxford University was able to write with bland self-assurance that African history before the arrival of Europeans had been nothing more than "blank, uninteresting, brutal barbarism." The professor's remark was published when the British Empire was at its height, and it represented a point of view that sought to justify the exploitation of Africans. If, as the professor claimed, Africans had lived in a state of chaos throughout their history, then the European domination of Africa was surely a blessing. As Europeans imposed their own government, religion, and social system upon Africans, the conquerors could believe that they were doing a noble service.

These views held sway into the 20th century. It was not until the end of World War II in 1945, when Africans began to break away from the European powers and form independent nations, that a sizable group of scholars began to take a fresh look at the African past. As archaeologists (scientists who study the physical remains of past societies) explored the sites of former African cities, they found evidence of a high level of civilization, thus confirming the observations of Mungo Park and other unbiased travelers. Not only had this civilization existed hundreds of years before the arrival of Europeans, but in many respects, the kingdoms and cities of Africa had reached a level of sophistication equal to or greater than that of European societies during the same period. The history of the West African kingdoms offers an intriguing view of a rich and long-neglected world and fascinating evidence of the vast range of human achievements.

MILESTONES
750-1900

c. 750 • The Soninke found ancient Ghana and gain power in the region by making iron weapons. Ancient Ghana emerges as a major trading state in the Sudan, controlling both the salt and the gold trades.

9th century • The Yoruba and Hausa states and the state of Kanem are established.

10th and 11th centuries • Ghana reaches the height of its wealth and power, impressing visitors with the grandeur of its cities. To manage this large kingdom, Ghana's king appoints princes to run its various provinces, creating a system similar to the states of medieval Europe.

1070 • Almoravids, fundamentalist Muslims from the Sahara, invade Ghana.

12th century • Ghana declines as a power in West Africa; the focus of trade shifts to Kangaba, a kingdom in the far south of the former Ghanaian empire.

1221-59 • Dunama Dibbelimi reigns in Kanem, which develops into a major power stretching from Lake Chad to North Africa; eventually the empire becomes Kanem-Bornu.

1240 • Sundiata defeats Sumanguru and becomes king of Kangaba, which grows into the Muslim empire of Mali.

1312–37 • Mansa Musa rules Mali, expanding its wealth and influence. Though respectful of traditional West African ways, he brings experts from Cairo to create Muslim schools and law courts and to introduce new building techniques.

c. 1400 • Dissatisfied with Mali's weak ruler, Gao declares its independence, leading to the rise of Songhay.

c. 1440
- Ewuare becomes oba (king) of the commercially prosperous Benin and unites its people into a powerful empire.

c. 1460-92
- Songhay ruler Sunni Ali, a great general, gains control of the entire middle Niger region, developing new farming methods and beginning a professional navy.

1472
- Portuguese sailors navigate the West African coast for the first time, making contact with Benin.

1493-1528
- Askia Muhammad governs Songhay, instituting Muslim practices and modernizing the government and military; Timbuktu and Jenne prosper as centers of learning and trade.

16th century
- By trading its highly valued textiles and metalwork, Oyo becomes the most powerful Yoruba state and dominates its neighbors. Barkwa Turunda and her daughter, Queen Amina, lead Zaria to dominance among the Hausa states.

1504
- Oba Esigie begins his reign as ruler of Benin and soon establishes a monopoly on trade with the English and Dutch.

1508-1617
- Idris Alooma rules the vast empire of Kanem-Bornu.

1590
- Seeking riches, the Moroccans invade Songhay; they succeed largely because they are armed with muskets.

c. 1695
- A unified Asante kingdom emerges under the leadership of Osei Tutu, who uses traditional religious beliefs to bring his people together.

Early 18th century
- Asante conquers Denkyira and takes over trade relations with the Europeans. The transatlantic slave trade begins to deform the societies of West Africa, depriving their economy of skilled workers and altering the balance of their political systems.

c. 1720-50   • Opoku Ware leads the expansion of Asante, gaining control of the Middle Niger trade routes.

1770-90   • Its leaders hampered by illiteracy, Oyo begins to decline in the unstable atmosphere of the slave trade; by 1840, its fall from power is complete.

1800-1850   • Seeking to create the ideal Islamic state, Uthman Dan Fodio leads the Fulani takeover of Kanem-Bornu and the Hausa states; the Sefawa dynasty falls after a record 1,000 years of stable rule in Kanem. Uthman's son, Sultan Muhammad Bello, unites the Hausa states but shatters the democratic element of the reform movement.

1824   • Provoked by the British governor's attempts to break their control of the region, Asante soldiers defeat the British in battle.

1874   • British forces invade Asante. The Treaty of Fomena, which gives the British free reign along the coast, marks the decline of Asante's power.

1884-85   • The European powers agree to divide up Africa, beginning decades of colonial rule.

1900   • The British occupy Asante, dissolving the last of the great West African kingdoms.

1

THE CRADLE
OF HUMANITY

THROUGHOUT the 20th century, scientists searching for the origins of the human race have turned more and more to the distant past of Africa. Increasingly, they have followed the trail blazed by Dr. Louis S. B. Leakey (1903–72). Based on work conducted in Kenya and Tanzania between the 1930s and the 1960s, Leakey concluded that Africa had been the setting for three all-important beginnings in human history. He claimed, first of all, that the basic stock of primates (an order of mammals that includes apes, monkeys, and human beings) originated in Africa about 30 or 40 million years ago. Then, according to Leakey, the main branch of human ancestors developed from the apes some 12 million years ago. Finally, the earliest members of the human race, *Homo sapiens*, made their home in Africa about 150,000 years ago and gradually spread from Africa to the rest of the globe.

Few scientists would argue with Leakey's first two conclusions; on the third proposition, some scholars contend that the first human beings did not originate in one particular area but in a number of locations,

This skillfully rendered terra-cotta head was found during excavations near the village of Nok, Nigeria, in the 1930s. The sculpture is a product of the so-called Nok culture, which flourished between 900 B.C. and A.D. 200.

Mount Cameroon rises above the grasslands near the Gulf of Guinea, southeast of Nigeria. In dramatic contrast to the Sahara Desert, which borders West Africa to the north, the region at the base of this mountain averages more than 400 inches of rainfall annually.

including the Middle East and Asia as well as Africa. This is a complicated subject, and the issue may be debated for many years to come. However, whether Africa is considered the single starting point of contemporary humanity or merely one among several, its central importance in human history is beyond dispute.

Africa is a huge continent, nearly 12 million square miles in area, a land that has always severely

challenged the people who have tried to put down roots in its vast expanses. The historian Basil Davidson, in his book *The African Genius*, has provided a vivid description of those challenges:

> There are deserts large enough to swallow half the lands of Europe, where intense heat by day gives way to bitter cold by night, and along whose stony boundaries the grasslands run out and disappear through skylines trembling in a distance eternally flat. There are great forests and wood-

lands where the sheer abundance of nature is clearly over-whelming in tall crops of grass that cut like knives, in thorns which catch and hold like hooks of steel, in a myriad marching ants and flies and creeping beasts that bite and itch and nag, in burning heat which sucks and clogs or rains that fall by slow gigantic torrents out of endless skies. . . . There are fine and temperate uplands, tall mountains, rugged hills, but even these are filled with an extravagance of nature.

For thousands of years, the first residents of Africa had no permanent cities or settlements. Instead, they moved from place to place, hunting wild animals and gathering plants for food. When the animals moved to new habitats or the plants in a region died out, the people were forced to find new locations in order to survive. The tools they used were made of stone, and thus the earliest period of human history is now known as the Stone Age.

About 6,000 years ago, human beings began plowing the earth with their stone implements and planting seeds that would produce edible foods. Human beings were able to remain in stable communities, many of them clustered in the fertile valley of the Nile River in east-central Africa. Other communities sprang up to the west, in what is now the vast Sahara Desert: throughout most of the period from 10,000 B.C. to 2500 B.C., the Sahara was a green and fertile area. These early farming communities—arising during the period known as the New Stone Age, or the Neolithic period—were the true beginning of human civilization.

A great change occurred in the life of these early communities about 2,500 years ago. At that time, human beings discovered how to extract iron ore from the earth: when heated in a fire, the iron could be shaped into tools and weapons. The coming of the Iron Age quickly changed the way people lived. Iron implements were much sharper and stronger than those made of stone and bone. With iron plows and

RECENT NEOLITHS

PLEISTOCENE PALEOLITHS

iron axes, humans could clear and cultivate larger areas of land than they had previously, and their communities expanded. Moreover, groups that possessed iron spears and swords were able to conquer other peoples equipped only with more primitive weapons. As a result, humanity spread out across Africa: by the beginning of the Christian era, all the

Until about 2,500 years ago, human beings made most of their tools from stone. This display of Stone Age implements is drawn mainly from the Neolithic period, during which humans learned to cultivate the soil.

The features of this Nok sculpture, part of a collection in the Jos Museum in Nigeria, are characteristically graceful and expressive.

regions of the continent were fully settled by the ancestors of modern-day Africans—though the total population of 3 or 4 million was a far cry from the 485 million of the late 20th century.

With the use of iron, society became more complicated. The early Stone Age communities were usually organized into clans—groups based on descent from a common ancestor. The head of the largest clan would often be the leader of the community. Thus the division of society tended to be vertical, with the elder members ruling the younger.

With the coming of the Iron Age, however, a horizontal division of society occurred as well. For one thing, larger communities were often more difficult to govern, so more organization was needed. In addition, people were now performing many different functions besides farming: communities included craftspeople, laborers, warriors, and traders. The inhabitants of Iron Age communities became more aware of their relation to one another and to the outside world. They saw themselves not only as the descendants of their ancestors but also as people who performed a function in society.

A leading example of the change in outlook that occurred between the Stone Age and the Iron Age is provided by remnants of the Nok culture. Little is known about the way the Nok people lived, but their artistic skill is evidenced in the clay figures they left behind, discovered in the 1930s during tin-mining operations near the village of Nok in Nigeria. The Nok sculptures, modeled in terra-cotta, a form of clay that can be heated to a lasting hardness, have been dated by scientists as extending in origin from 900 B.C. to A.D. 200, thus spanning the range of both the Stone Age and the Iron Age.

The sculptures consist mostly of human faces. As Basil Davidson has written in *Africa in History,* "These figures are remarkable for their great artistic qualities, combining . . . a rare sensitivity to human character and features with a sophistication of style that seems extraordinary for the times in which they were made." They show that West Africans had already become vividly aware of the world they lived in, so much so that they felt the need to record their impressions in a form that would last for centuries. This occurred at a time when art was virtually nonexistent in many parts of Europe.

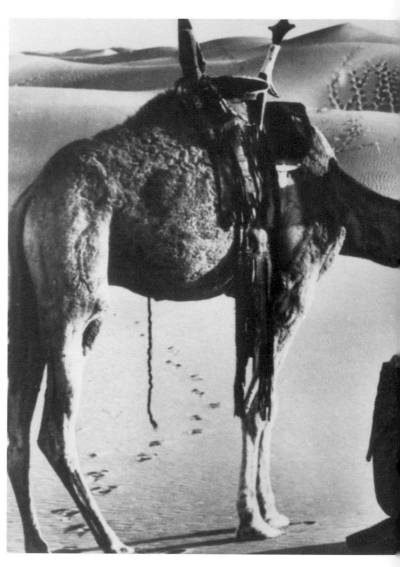

Muslim travelers stop to pray as they journey across the Sahara, the world's largest desert.

Despite the example of Nok, West Africa's location caused it to lag behind the eastern and northern regions of the continent. While West Africans were still living in farming settlements, the Egyptians, in contact with the great river-valley civilizations of the Near East, such as Babylon and Assyria, enjoyed a culture of high sophistication under their rulers, the pharaohs. The communities of North Africa, propelled into close contact with the Romans and Phoe-

nicians by their position on the Mediterranean Sea, were large and prosperous by the 4th century B.C.

West Africa was separated from these civilizations by the Sahara, a 3-million-square-mile expanse of land that, by around 2000 B.C., had dried to desert. This geographic barrier did not prevent the development of West Africa during the Iron Age. South of the Sahara and extending all the way from the Atlantic Ocean to the Gulf of Aden in the Middle

East was a vast plain commonly referred to as the African savanna. Though this plain contained different environments—some dry and open, some moist and wooded—it was, until it merged with dense tropical rain forests along the coast, an area that was both friendly to human settlement and easy to travel through. As the archaeologist Graham Connah has pointed out in his 1987 book, *African Civilizations*, the region's very diversity aided its development:

> Each environment possessed some resources but lacked others. Thus salt was available in the desert and along the coast but was relatively difficult to obtain in the savanna. . . . Thus the forest was deficient in meat but the savanna supported very large numbers of domestic animals. There are many other examples that could be given to illustrate this situation but the important point is that the complexity of the West African environment, as a whole, provided conditions conducive to the development of a complex network of regional trade. . . . It is quite likely that such trading activity was almost as old as West African food production and the beginnings of a trading network could well have been already in existence by about three thousand years ago.

However, one of the most important links in that trading network, the journey back and forth through the Sahara, was truly challenging. Because temperatures in the Sahara, the world's largest desert, can reach as high as 120 degrees Fahrenheit and supplies of water are scant, the trans-Sahara journey required courage, determination, and careful planning. Travelers who became separated from their companions seldom emerged alive.

By the 7th century A.D., trading caravans from North African cities such as Marrakesh, Fez, Algiers, Tunis, and Tripoli frequently made the daunting journey through the desert. Other caravans came from Cairo in the east. The trek became easier when camels began to replace horses, because camels are able to travel long distances without water, and their wider hooves make it easier for them to move through sand. In addition to salt, the caravans brought copper, silks, and other metalware to the West Africans, who provided textiles, nuts, spices, ironwork, and gold in exchange.

As the trade routes flourished, the settlements of West Africa began more and more to resemble their counterparts to the north and east in size, wealth, and splendor. Before long, they would be equal to any of the cities in the world.

2

THE LAND OF GOLD

THE first of the great trading empires to emerge in West Africa was ancient Ghana. Ancient Ghana occupied a large territory that lay between the Senegal River and the western branch of the Niger River. This territory was well inland and thus entirely distinct from the modern-day nation of Ghana, which is situated on the coast, bordering the Gulf of Guinea. Ancient Ghana was founded at least as early as A.D. 750 by a people known as the Soninke; some scholars believe that the date of founding may have been as many as 500 years earlier. In any case, Ghana had emerged as a major trading power by the year 800.

The Soninke originally called their state Wagadu. The term *ghana*, which means "war chief" in the Mande language, was originally used to describe one of the functions of the king. Gradually, no doubt owing to the importance of military power in main-

The homes of ancient Ghana resembled the architecture of this 20th-century African village, constructed of clay and covered with thatched roofs.

Residents of the ancient city of Timbuktu carry goods past a mosque.

taining the state, the term came to replace the nation's original name.

A second title held by the king of Ghana was *kaya maghan*, "master of the gold." The king's two most important functions, leadership in war and control over the gold trade, indicate why the Soninke found it desirable to be led by a single individual rather than a group of clan chiefs. In order to control neighboring peoples, the Soninke needed unified military forces; when dealing with trading partners, it was an advantage to have a unified economic policy.

The power of the Soninke was really based on their superior skill in working iron. Equipped with iron-pointed spears, Ghana's armies easily subdued the forces of their West African neighbors, who fought with much less efficient weapons made of stone, bone, and wood. However, Ghana itself was not the source of the gold eagerly sought by traders from North Africa and Egypt. The precious substance derived from the forest belt to the south of Ghana, where there were rich gold deposits and a population skilled in mining. By controlling the territory that lay between the producers of the gold and those who wished to acquire it, Ghana made itself a crucial element in the trading process.

Ghana was able to control the flow of gold from south to north, and Ghanaians also controlled the north-to-south flow of salt, a precious commodity for which West Africans were ready to trade their gold. For each donkey-load of salt that entered Ghana from the north, the king collected an import tax of one *mitqal,* equal to one-eighth of an ounce of gold. For each donkey-load of salt that left Ghana for the south, the king collected an export tax of two mitqals from Ghana's southern neighbors. In this manner, Ghana became known throughout Africa as the Land of Gold, without itself producing an ounce of the glittering metal.

Ghana also carefully regulated the flow of gold across its borders, making sure that the metal would not become so widely available that the price would drop. As the gold mines of central Europe were being rapidly exhausted, Ghana began to enjoy a monopoly on the gold trade. For this reason, any ruler who wished to obtain gold for the minting of coins could only obtain it from Ghana, by way of the North African traders.

The rulers of Ghana strived to live up to their role as masters of the gold trade, maintaining their kingdom at a level of grandeur that deeply impressed traders and other visitors. Many of these visitors wrote about what they saw, and the most reliable of their accounts were compiled during the 11th century by al-Bakri, an Arab writer living in the Spanish city of Córdoba. In al-Bakri's day, the king of Ghana was Tunka Manin, who, according to the writer, could "put two hundred thousand warriors in the field, more than forty thousand of them being armed with bow and arrow." No less impressive was the splendor of the royal court:

> When [the king] gives an audience to his people, to listen to their complaints and set them to rights, he sits in a pavilion around which stand his horses caparisoned in cloth of gold; behind him stand ten pages holding shields and gold-mounted swords; and on his right are the sons of the princes of his empire, splendidly clad and with gold plaited into their hair. The governor of the city is seated on the ground next to the king, and all around him are his counsellors in the same position. The gate of the chamber is guarded by dogs of an excellent breed. These dogs never leave the king's seat. They wear collars of gold and silver, ornamented with metals.

Other travelers reported, perhaps a bit more fancifully, that the king of Ghana held enormous banquets attended by thousands of guests and that he possessed a nugget of gold so large that he could tether his horse to it.

It is likely that the capital city moved several times during Ghana's history, but scholars believe that at the time of al-Bakri's account, the capital was Kumbi

The prophet Muhammad founded the religion of Islam during the 7th century A.D.

Saleh, whose ruins were first discovered in 1914. Throughout the following decades, archaeologists digging at the site reconstructed the outlines of a large city, whose population may have numbered as many as 30,000 people. Like most of West Africa's great trading centers, Kumbi Saleh comprised two separate settlements, one for Ghanaians and the other for visiting North African traders. The houses of the Ghanaians were built in the typical West African fashion, with circular walls of clay and cone-shaped thatched roofs. The North Africans usually built square houses from blocks of stone and finished the interior walls with yellow plaster. In two large mansions uncovered in Kumbi Saleh, archaeologists found a variety of finely made objects, including weapons, farming tools, glass weights for weighing gold, and fragments of pottery.

The upkeep of a city such as Kumbi Saleh, let alone an empire of Ghana's extent, required not only great wealth but also careful political organization. The king might control the gold trade, but with his subjects spread out over so large a territory, there was no way that he could hold all the power of government in his own hands. In order to convey orders, the king had to employ messengers who rode on horseback to far-flung communities. Given the distances involved and the hardships of travel, the network of messengers was not an efficient way of making the most basic day-to-day decisions.

Therefore, the king was obliged to appoint a series of princes to rule the provinces of the empire in his name. The princes had a wide range of power, but they were ultimately servants of the king, and all of them paid taxes to the central government. By instituting this form of political organization, Ghana made a dramatic departure from the previous communities of West Africa, placing itself on a par with the states of medieval Europe.

The rule of Ghana's Tunka Manin was similar in many ways to that of his European contemporary William the Conqueror, the French nobleman who seized control of England in 1066 and crowned himself King William I. Under the feudal system of government practiced by William, lords and vassals were bound together by ties of mutual loyalty. Vassals—in this case the barons of England—held their land by grant from King William; in return, they paid him taxes and pledged to support him in time of war. No baron had the right to wage war on his own, and all were compelled by various legal traditions to pledge their obedience to the king. The same principles prevailed in Ghana, with some important differences. William had invaded England with an estimated 5,000 men at arms, and he would undoubtedly have envied the 200,000 troops at the command of Tunka Manin—not to mention the splendor of Ghana's royal court and major cities.

In the course of history, however, ancient Ghana was not destined to achieve the same longevity as the nation of England. Like William the Conqueror, the rulers of Ghana did not believe in standing still. During the course of their history, they strove with some success to expand their borders. To the extent that they could gain control over both the gold-producing areas to the south and the salt-producing areas to the north, their wealth and power would steadily increase.

Ghana may have enjoyed a monopoly of the African gold trade, but it had no monopoly on the idea of

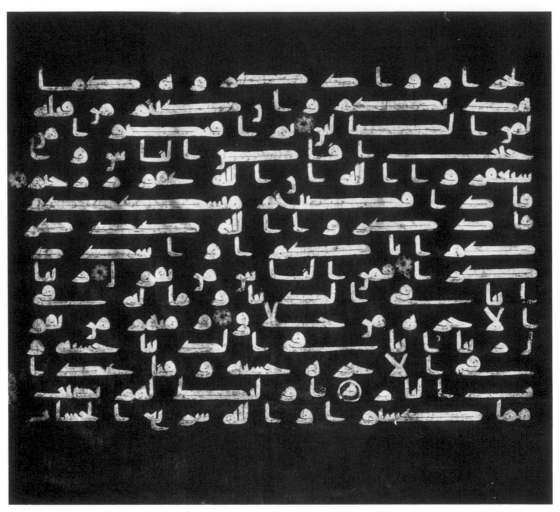

The Almoravids, who invaded Ghana in 1070, believed in strict adherence to the doctrines of the Koran, the sacred book of Islam. This page of text, a leaf of parchment inscribed in gold, is part of a 9th-century Koran from Kairouan, Tunisia.

expansion. That idea has been the common property of many nations and peoples. In the 11th century, one such group inspired by the dream of conquest was known as the Almoravids. Ghana eventually became their victim.

The Almoravids were as much a religious phenomenon as a political force. They were adherents of the religion of Islam, which had its origins in the deserts of Arabia, to the east of Africa, during the 7th century. At that time, the Arabian tribes worshiped a variety of gods, many of them associated with forces of nature. These beliefs competed with the teachings of both the Jewish and Christian religions, which centered upon a single god and a written code regulating the worship and conduct of believers.

In this context, the prophet Muhammad, an Arab tribesman who spent his early years as a caravan driver, developed the religion of Islam. Like Judaism and Christianity, Islam was based upon the worship of a single god, Allah. Similar to the Old Testament of Judaism and the New Testament of Christianity, the holy book known as the Koran contained the teachings of the new religion, which was in many respects far stricter in its demands upon worshipers.

Like most champions of new ideas, Muhammad met powerful resistance during his career as a prophet. But by the time of his death in A.D. 632, he had gained masses of followers who were eager to spread the faith. By the end of the 7th century, the Islamic Arabs, commonly known as Muslims, had swept through North Africa. In the early years of the 8th century, they crossed the Mediterranean and conquered most of Spain. It was only a matter of time before Islam exerted its power upon the rest of Africa.

The people known as Almoravids were, from the standpoint of the 11th century, newcomers in the Muslim world. They owed their origin to a Muslim holy man named Ibn Yasin, who traveled from Arabia to the Sahara Desert around 1039. Ibn Yasin had been summoned by a tribal leader who wished his people to receive religious instruction. As a fundamentalist, Ibn Yasin preached strict adherence to the doctrines of the Koran, which demanded frequent prayer and allowed very little in the way of personal enjoyment. This teaching was at odds with the general tone of Muslim civilization, especially in North Africa and Spain. In the conquered territories, Muslims had developed a graceful and enlightened culture that featured wide-ranging commerce, scholarship, science, and splendid works of art and architecture. The North Africans had little use for Ibn Yasin's harsh doctrines, and as soon as his sponsor died, they drove the teacher away.

Undeterred, Ibn Yasin traveled to the Atlantic coast and founded a religious community known as a *ribat*. He had great success in attracting followers, who became known in Arabic as *al-Murabitun*, "the people of the ribat," from which the name Almoravid was derived. When he had sufficient forces, Ibn Yasin conquered the Saharan tribes that had once rejected him, and he made himself master of the northern desert. Following Ibn Yasin's death in battle in 1059, the Almoravids eventually split into two groups. The northern group, under Yusuf ibn Tashufin, systematically conquered North Africa and then swept into Spain with the object of controlling the entire nation. The southern group, led by Abu Bakr, set its sights on Ghana.

Abu Bakr began his campaign against Ghana in 1070 by forming an alliance with the people of Takrur, a kingdom on the Atlantic coast. The Almoravids quickly captured and plundered Audoghast, one of Ghana's most important cities, located in the northwestern part of the empire. But Ghana's army was so powerful that Abu Bakr's forces were unable to capture Kumbi Saleh until 1076. By contrast, the Almoravid forces that invaded Spain made short work of a supposedly invincible Christian army at the Battle of Sagrajas in 1086. They seemed certain to conquer all of Spain until the warrior Rodrigo Díaz, known as El Cid, defeated them at the Battle of Cuarte in 1094.

In the end, the Almoravids could not hold on to their West African territories either. The proud Ghanaians staged continual revolts, and Abu Bakr himself was killed while fighting rebel forces in 1087. For two centuries thereafter, a number of neighboring states, including Takrur, tried to gain control of the territory of Ghana. None of their attempts was successful. But throughout all the region's political and military up-heavals, the western savanna continued to prosper. It was only a matter of time before a new empire took shape to recapture the grandeur of the Land of Gold.

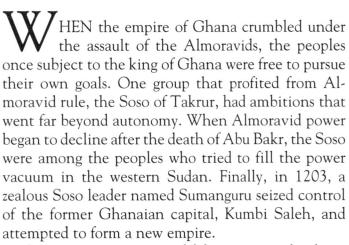

3

"WHERE THE KING RESIDES"

WHEN the empire of Ghana crumbled under the assault of the Almoravids, the peoples once subject to the king of Ghana were free to pursue their own goals. One group that profited from Almoravid rule, the Soso of Takrur, had ambitions that went far beyond autonomy. When Almoravid power began to decline after the death of Abu Bakr, the Soso were among the peoples who tried to fill the power vacuum in the western Sudan. Finally, in 1203, a zealous Soso leader named Sumanguru seized control of the former Ghanaian capital, Kumbi Saleh, and attempted to form a new empire.

Sumanguru was a powerful figure, reputed to have the gift of witchcraft for use against his enemies. But he soon found his drive for control of the western Sudan in serious jeopardy. For one thing, the Muslim traders who had been installed in Kumbi Saleh for centuries refused to accept his overlordship. They abandoned their settlement and traveled north to the

The village of Kirina, pictured here, was the site of a battle between rival kings Sundiata and Sumanguru in 1240.

37

This shrine is located in Kangaba, a small town on the upper Niger River that was once the capital of the Mandinka kingdom Kangaba. The building belongs to the Keita clan, of which the legendary Sundiata was a member, and dates from as early as the third century A.D.

edge of the Sahara, where they set up a new trading center at Walata. Thus, Sumanguru lost any chance of controlling the gold trade with North Africa.

An even more significant challenge to Sumanguru's ambitions came from the Mandinka people of Kangaba. Kangaba was a small state situated in the far south of the former empire of Ghana, but it had played an important part in the gold trade. Scholars believe that the Mandinka of Kangaba had journeyed to the gold country along the Senegal River and transported the precious metal to the trading centers of Ghana. In addition, the Mandinka had long been skilled in farming, cultivating rice and other valuable crops in the fertile land occupied by Kangaba. For this reason, their population increased steadily through the years, and their importance in the politics of the region grew.

Like the Muslim traders, the Mandinka found
Sumanguru's regime difficult to deal with. His taxes
were burdensome, and he failed to maintain law
and order in his dominions, with the result that the
caravan routes were plagued by bandits. Sumanguru
also considered it his privilege to carry off Mandinka
women. Kangaba seethed with the spirit of revolt, but
the Mandinka's king lacked the courage to lead them.
When he realized that Sumanguru was preparing to
move against him, he fled and left his people to fend
for themselves.

The Mandinka found their savior in the deposed
king's half brother, Sundiata Keita. According to oral
traditions that still survive in West Africa, Sundiata
was born lame but was cured by a miracle, with the
aid of the royal blacksmith. He became a great hunter
and warrior, but he had to go into exile to escape the
anger of the king's principal wife, who feared that
Sundiata would rival her own son for the throne.
Sundiata now returned home and gathered an army
to confront Sumanguru. The two sides met in battle
at Kirina in 1240. As the battle is now recalled, both
leaders employed their supernatural powers. The army
of Sumanguru appeared on the horizon in the shape
of a cloud, and Sundiata's army took the form
of a mountain.

Sundiata's powers proved greater. He knew that
Sumanguru, like all warriors, was protected by magic
only against wounds from iron. Sundiata prepared a
poison and injected the venom into the claw of a
white rooster: when one of the Mandinka warriors
shot Sumanguru with an arrow tipped with this claw,
Sumanguru's magic deserted him and he vanished
from the face of the earth. Sundiata now took control
of Sumanguru's former territory and appointed Mandinka leaders to govern the various provinces. The
little state of Kangaba now emerged as the center of a

new empire, which soon became known as Mali, meaning "where the king resides."

The rulers of Mali adopted the title *mansa*, which means "lord" in the Mandinka language. They occupied the same position as the former kings of Ghana, with one significant difference: the lords of Mali were all Muslims.

Abu Bakr, the leader of the Almoravids, had not merely been seeking riches and territory when he invaded ancient Ghana. He also sought to forcibly convert West Africans to the religion of Islam. Combined with the influence exerted by the long-established presence of Muslim traders from North Africa, Islam had a powerful impact on West Africa, at least among the ruling classes. It is safe to conclude that the majority of the people continued to follow their traditional religions, which had much in common with the religions practiced in the Middle East before the coming of Islam. Nature worship and the belief in spirits were important ingredients of the ancient creeds. Animals were often given the status of gods; in West Africa, the snake and the ram had particular power. For the average West African, these age-old beliefs, centered upon the land and all its inhabitants, appeared to provide greater meaning and comfort than the more complicated ideas of Islam. The notion of a single god who had no real earthly form, not to mention a holy book written in an unfamiliar language, could not have had great appeal to the people of the African countryside.

According to Basil Davidson, the actual founders of West African states, such as Sundiata, well understood the need to combine political achievements with long-held beliefs. In his book *Africa in History*, Davidson points out that Sundiata's conversion to Islam was undoubtedly a gesture of goodwill toward the Muslim traders; to his own people he presented himself as a champion of traditional religion, "a

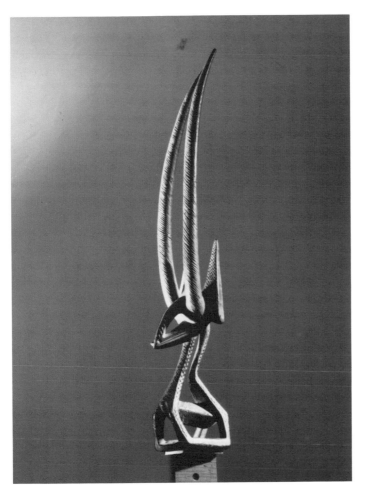

This dance headdress, a creation of the Bambara tribe in Mali, represents Tyi-wara, a mythical figure whose name means "farmer with the strength of a wild animal." Half-man and half-antelope, Tyi-wara is credited with teaching the Bambara their agricultural skills.

powerful man of magic or enchantment." For later rulers, on the other hand, the unifying principles of Islam, and the rich culture that had been built upon it, offered a promise of growth and stability that proved irresistible. Sundiata's successors, therefore, gradually turned away from the ancient traditions. They set about making Mali a great Muslim empire, and they succeeded brilliantly.

Perhaps the greatest of all the lords of Mali was Mansa Musa, who ruled from 1312 to 1337. Under his regime, the borders of Mali expanded

in all directions, encompassing more trade routes, more wealth-producing areas, and the thriving cities of Gao and Timbuktu along the Niger. Consequently, in 1324, when Mansa Musa embarked on a pilgrimage to Mecca, the holy city of Islam, he caused a stir in the Muslim world that gave rise to long-lasting tales of grandeur. He was said to have taken more than 500 slaves with him, each one of them carrying a staff of solid gold. (Basil Davidson points out that present-day chiefs in West Africa still have ceremonial parades with golden staffs, though the staffs are now made of wood and simply decorated with gold.) When the great lord passed through Cairo, he gave so much gold to the residents that the price of the commodity fell and the whole economy of the city was affected.

Mansa Musa's experiences in Cairo and Mecca inspired him to rival the Muslim princes of the East, not only in wealth but also in culture and good works. He returned from his pilgrimage with a number of Egyptian scholars, who set up schools and law courts. The Muslim schools, famed throughout the world for their superb quality, had a major impact on West Africa, where scholarship had not previously been promoted. Because the religion of Islam centered upon the study and observance of the Koran, reading and writing were all-important, and more and more Muslim West Africans began to acquire these skills.

Islamic law courts were also distinctive in applying the commandments of the Koran to every aspect of life. Muslim judges, called *qadis*, possessed wide-ranging powers to inflict punishment, including the death penalty, on offenders. Such strict measures were foreign to the African law administered by tribal elders. In Africa, as in other societies whose religious beliefs are closely tied to nature (such as those of the North American Indians), the death penalty was rarely applied. Even in cases of murder, the judgment usually involved a payment of goods or livestock to the victim's family. Thus, the emphasis was on restoring balance in a practical sense rather than fulfilling a principle of justice: taking "an eye for an eye" might be morally satisfying, but a gift of cattle would put food in the mouths of a family that had lost one of its providers.

Mansa Musa, understanding how deeply his people were wedded to their traditional religion and ways of life, was careful to maintain the old religion and law side by side with the new Muslim institutions. For example, the Muslim traveler al-Bakri noted that there were areas in Mali to be avoided: "Around the king's town are domed huts and groves where live the sorcerers, the men in charge of their religious cult. In these are also the idols and the tombs of their kings. These groves are guarded, no one can enter them nor discover their contents. The prisons of the king are there, and if anyone is imprisoned in them, no more is ever heard of him."

Mansa Musa had brought architects as well as scholars back from Cairo, and before long his builders had erected a magnificent mosque (Islamic house of worship) in Timbuktu and a new royal palace in the capital city of Niani. Mansa Musa also introduced new building techniques for ordinary houses. Instead of the traditional round structures with clay walls and conical thatched roofs, the people of Mali now became accustomed to brick houses with flat roofs.

Like the kings of ancient Ghana, Mansa Musa appointed governors to rule Mali's various provinces. Mali went a step further, though, by surrounding the king with a group of advisers who roughly corresponded to the cabinet ministers of later centuries. In the capital, there was a minister known as the

The principal mosque of Timbuktu, built during the reign of the Malian king Mansa Musa, is the oldest surviving mosque in West Africa.

hari-farma who was in charge of regulating all the fishing in the Niger River; the *sao-farma* supervised all of Mali's forests; the *babili-farma* was in charge of agriculture; and the *khalissi-farma* took care of the empire's financial affairs.

Apparently, most of these officials performed their duties well. The often chaotic and dangerous conditions that had plagued the western Sudan after the decline of ancient Ghana gave way to a reign of peace

and prosperity. Ibn Battuta, a Muslim scholar who traveled widely throughout Africa and Asia during the 14th century, visited Mali 12 years after Mansa Musa's death and found that the ruler had created a state of "complete and general safety." At the court of Mansa Suleyman, Musa's successor, Ibn Battuta was confronted by a splendid spectacle:

> The lord of this kingdom has a great balcony in his palace. There he has a great seat of ebony that is like a throne fit for a large and tall person. It is flanked by elephants' tusks. The king's arms stand near him. They are all of gold; sword and lance, bow and quiver of arrows. . . . Before him stand about twenty Turkish or other pages, who are brought from Cairo. One of these, standing on his left, holds a silk umbrella that is topped by a dome and bird of gold. The bird is like a hawk. The king's officers are seated in a circle near him, in two rows, one to the right and one to the left. Beyond them sit the commanders of the cavalry. In front of him there is a person who never leaves him and who is his executioner; and another who is his official spokesman, and who is named the herald. In front of him there are also drummers. Others dance before their king and make him merry.

As he traveled throughout Mali, Ibn Battuta found much more to marvel at, including the beauty and manners of the women, who were treated with great respect and did not follow the Muslim practice of covering their faces in the presence of men.

He also noted that the people of Mali were very free in sexual matters, with married men and women often having "companions" outside the family. The learned traveler wrote:

> A man may go into his house and find his wife entertaining her "companion," but he takes no objection to it. One day at Walata I went into the qadi's house . . . and found him with a young woman of remarkable beauty. When I saw her I was shocked and turned to go out, but she laughed at me, instead of being overcome with shame, and the qadi

said to me "Why are you going out? She is my companion."
I was amazed at their conduct, for he was a theologian and
a pilgrim to boot. I was told that he had asked the sultan's
permission to make the pilgrimage [to Mecca] that year
with his "companion" (whether this one or not I cannot
say) but the sultan would not grant it.

Compared with this prosperous, cultured, and sophisticated society, 14th-century Europe was hardly
impressive. During that period, European life was
dominated by the Hundred Years' War, a long series
of conflicts between France and England over England's territorial claims in France. The war, which
raged on and off between 1337 and 1453, devastated
much of France. Meanwhile, all of Europe was swept
by the Black Death, an outbreak of bubonic plague
that wiped out one-third of the continent's population by 1350. Peasant revolts broke out in France and
England; learning and culture declined with the death
of Europe's leading scholars; religious life was disrupted and fanatical sects began to flourish as large
segments of the clergy succumbed to the plague.
Nothing could have been farther removed from the
peaceful, prosperous cities of Mali, with their mosques
and new brick houses, their markets filled with goods,
the canoes in the river Niger, and the great caravans
coming in from the Sahara.

As it turned out, much of Mali's stability rested
upon the leadership of Mansa Musa. Most of his
successors were lesser men. Mansa Suleyman, who
ruled during the time of Ibn Battuta's visit, managed
to continue the great tradition, but after his death in
1360, the throne was occupied by a succession of rulers
who were both inept and unpopular. The strain on the
empire became apparent after 1400, when the city of
Gao proclaimed its independence and refused to pay
taxes to the emperor. At the same time, the ever-
dangerous Tuaregs swept in from the Sahara and

captured both Walata and Timbuktu. In the west, the Wolof people began to build their own empire. Mali did not collapse; the respect and honor its emperors had earned still remained throughout the western Sudan, even as the empire's power and wealth declined. But after 200 years, it was time for other peoples to occupy center stage—in a process that unfolded, next to the violent convulsions of Europe, like a great historical pageant.

4

SONGHAY

AMONG the great conquests of Mali was the thriving city of Gao on the Niger River. The city had been founded in the 7th century by the Songhay, a race of energetic traders. By the beginning of the 11th century, when the Songhay king Kossoi converted to Islam, Gao was a major terminus for the great caravans making their way south through the Sahara (a position Gao still occupies today). Early in the 14th century, Gao's prosperity made the city a ripe target for the lords of Mali, and for decades its citizens submitted to their rule. But after the decline of Mali's military power, the Songhay people began their own program of expansion. By the time they were done, their empire had become the largest ever known in West Africa.

> **The rise of the Songhay empire to greatness began in the 1460s with the reign of Sunni (King) Ali, a leader whose deeds are still spoken of in the villages of West Africa. Sunni Ali was**

The city of Jenne, situated on the Bani River, a tributary of the Niger, was taken by the Songhay leader Sunni Ali in the 1470s. Long established as an important trading center, Jenne flourished throughout the Songhay empire, serving as a link between the traders of Timbuktu and the gold producers of the southern forest belt.

49

above all a great general, and his skills as a commander were in constant demand. While the Songhay had been subject to the king of Mali, their tax payments had at least purchased peace and stability. Now, with Mali's forces no longer present to maintain order, the Songhay were pressed on all sides by hostile forces. One by one, Sunni Ali eliminated these threats; the rise of the Songhay empire was due mostly to his victories on the battlefield.

Sunni Ali began by defeating the Mossi, the Dogon, and the Fulani, all formidable warrior groups of the western Sudan. Then he recaptured Timbuktu from the Tuareg raiders of the Sahara, who had seized the city in 1433. Following the course of the Niger River to the west, Sunni Ali then assaulted Jenne, a vital trading center. No attacker had ever been able to take the city, but Sunni Ali patiently besieged it for seven years and captured it in 1476. Eight years after ascending the throne, Sunni Ali had the entire middle Niger region under his control.

Following the pattern of other West African leaders who founded great empires, Sunni Ali was a traditionalist in matters of religion. He was wise enough to pay elaborate respects to the Muslim faith of his trading partners, but he knew that his power rested primarily on the support of the farmers and fishermen of the Niger grasslands; like Sundiata Keita and other founding fathers, he was known primarily as a champion of the old religion. His preference became especially clear in times of crisis. For example, when he recaptured Timbuktu, he confronted the Muslim community with the charge of disloyalty, alleging that they had delivered the city into the hands of the

Tuareg raiders. He then punished the qadis with such severity that the Muslims of Timbuktu thought of him long afterward as a cruel tyrant. But his actions no doubt won the approval of the non-Muslims in the countryside, and experience had clearly taught him that this was the true basis of power in West Africa. Without question, prosperity came from the Muslims of the cities, but the military strength that made peaceful commerce possible depended on the rugged folk of the hinterland, who formed the core of the king's army.

By the time Sunni Ali died in 1492, the Songhay empire surpassed both of its great predecessors, Ghana and Mali. Not only did Sunni Ali conquer and restore order to the Sudan, but he also proved a brilliant administrator. He created provinces where none had existed before, developed new methods of farming, and organized the boatmen of the Niger into the beginnings of a professional navy.

Sunni Ali's son, Sunni Baru, inherited his father's crown but could not recapture the elder man's aura of success. Within a year of taking over the throne, Baru had a serious rebellion on his hands. The root of the problem was his failure to follow his father in bridging the gap between town and country. Rather than paying court both to Islamic traders and practitioners of the old religion, Baru declared that he was a devotee of Songhay's traditional beliefs and that he wanted nothing to do with Islam. Though he correctly understood the basis of his power, he clearly underestimated the risks involved in taking sides so openly.

The Muslims of the towns had endured Sunni Ali's punishments because they had been reassured by his public respect for their religion and his recognition of their importance to the welfare of Songhay. Baru's open hostility, on the other hand, convinced them that they were in danger of losing their influence in the royal court. It would then be only a matter of time before they lost their trading privileges and their wealth. Believing that they now had nothing to lose by rebelling against the king, the Muslims found a leader in Muhammad Turay, a high-ranking army official. Only 14 months into Sunni Baru's reign, Muhammad Turay defeated him in battle and replaced him on the throne.

Muhammad Turay, who became known as Askia Muhammad, ruled from 1493 to 1528. His decision to take the title *askia*, a military rank in the Songhay army, rather than the traditional royal title *sunni*, was an indication of his intention to break with the past. Indeed, his reign brought about a dramatic shift in power from the countryside to the cities, where his support was strongest. Though he did not repeat the error of Sunni Baru by turning his back on a whole segment of Songhay's population, Askia Muhammad's actions made it plain to all that his adherence to Islam was more than a political gesture.

Almost immediately after his victory over Sunni Baru, Askia Muhammad set out on a two-year pilgrimage to Mecca. When he returned home, he began instituting Muslim laws and practices wherever possible, relying on the advice of a North African sage named al-Maghili. By 1500, Leo Africanus, a widely traveled Muslim writer, was able to record the following impression of Timbuktu: "There are many judges, professors, and holy men, all being generously helped by the king, who holds scholars in much honor. Here, too, they sell many handwritten books from North Africa. More profit is made from selling books in Timbuktu than from any other branch of trade."

Askia Muhammad also went further than any previous West African ruler in the organization of his realm. His most important innovation was to open up the ranks of government service. Previously, governors and other leading officials had been appointed on the basis of their birth: they were all heads of

The ancient mosque of Jenne, a major center of Muslim learning during the height of the Songhay empire, looms above an open square.

important clans or descent lines. Askia Muhammad, while honoring the traditional methods, also followed the Muslim principle of equality, which valued learning and piety more than birth. Under Muhammad, able men could achieve high office regardless of their social position.

Askia Muhammad divided his empire into five provinces, each one headed by a governor: Kurmina, Dendi, Baro, Dirma, and Bangu. The central government, based in Gao, consisted of many war chiefs and civil chiefs; most of these chiefs, as in the case of Mali, bore the title *farma*. Askia Muhammad, however, was not content to have a single official in charge of each important governmental function. He also appointed a host of subofficials, creating a structure much like the system of ministers, secretaries, and undersecretaries of modern nations. For example, Songhay's *katisi-farma*, or finance minister, was assisted by the *waney-farma*, who handled all questions of property; the *bara-farma*, who looked after the payment of wages; and the *dey-farma*, who was in charge of all

purchasing done by the government. Other depart-
ments were divided along similar lines.

Askia Muhammad also took great pains to mod-
ernize his military forces, building on the work of
Sunni Ali. Previously, the kings of West Africa had
relied upon the traditions of feudalism in times of war,
calling upon their vassals to provide fighting men.
There had been no such thing as a standing army at
the command of the king. The advantage of this
system was largely economic—the king was spared the
expense of housing and feeding a large body of soldiers, and in times of peace the soldiers were free to
pursue other occupations. On the other hand, the
feudal system caused inevitable delays in gathering
and deploying forces. During the 15th and 16th centuries, when African rulers were developing more
sophisticated methods of warfare, training and discipline became more important than ever before. A
body of amateur soldiers quickly brought together
would not have the same prowess in battle as would a
group of veterans who enjoyed the benefit of constant
training.

Askia Muhammad therefore organized a permanent professional army, under a general who bore the
title *dyini-koy*. The king also created a full-time navy
made up of Niger boatmen, who served under an
admiral known as the *hi-koy*. A third official, the
tara-farma, was in charge of Songhay's cavalry.

Under Askia Muhammad's administration, the
cities of Songhay reached their full flowering. Timbuktu, because of its vulnerability to the Tuareg raiders of the Sahara, never became a leading political
center. But, as Leo Africanus noted admiringly, the
city was a center of religion and learning, and it
produced a number of native-born writers who left
valuable records in Arabic of the Songhay empire.
One of these writers, Ahmed Baba, created a number
of works that—according to Basil Davidson—are still

in use among the Muslims of West Africa. Muhammad Kati, born in Timbuktu in 1468, began his great
work, *Tarikh al Fattash* (The History of the Seeker of
Knowledge), in 1519. As a member of Askia Muhammad's personal staff, Kati accompanied the emperor
to Mecca and was thus in a unique position to record
the development of Songhay. Reputedly, he lived to
the age of 125; his sons and grandsons continued the
Tarikh al Fattash, bringing the work to completion in
1665.

As in the case of earlier empires, the culture and
organization of Songhay depended finally upon the
trade that flourished in its cities. In addition to Gao
and Timbuktu, the city of Jenne played a significant
role in the prosperity of the empire. Located farther
west along the Niger, Jenne served as a link between
the traders of Timbuktu and the gold producers of
the southern forest belt. As Nehemiah Levtzion has
pointed out in his book *Ancient Ghana and Mali*, great
blocks of salt were transported by canoe from Timbuktu to Jenne, where they were broken up into
smaller pieces and carried by porters to the goldfields
of the south. Jenne's bustling trade was carried on by
the same Mandinka people who had been responsible
for the founding of the kingdom of Mali: they had
centered their operations in Jenne since the decline
of the Mali empire. The city itself, protected by its
location in the flood plain of the Niger and by a high
defensive wall, had never been under the control of
Mali; it had remained independent until it was taken
by Sunni Ali in the 1470s. During the 17th century,
the scholar al-Sa'di described the city in terms that
certainly would have applied during the heyday of
Songhay: "This city is large, flourishing, and prosperous. . . . Jenne is one of the great markets of the Muslim
world. There one meets the salt merchants from the
mines of Teghaza and merchants carrying gold from
the mines of Bitou. . . . Because of this blessed city,

This terra-cotta sculpture, found during excavations near Jenne, may have been produced as early as the 1300s. The snake on the figure's forehead suggests its connection with the Niger belt's traditional religions, which have deep ties to the animal world.

caravans flock to Timbuktu from all points of the horizon. . . . The area around Jenne is fertile and well populated; with numerous markets held there on all the days of the week. It is certain that it contains 7,077 villages very near to one another."

Though Jenne was a flourishing Muslim center in the Songhay empire and continues to function today in the republic of Mali, with its ancient mosque still in use, archaeologists have concluded from examining ancient burial sites that the city was originally founded by non-Islamic Africans who observed the traditional religions. It appears that the city owed its initial rise—at least as early as A.D. 1000—to the fertility of the Niger flood plain, which made it possible for the inhabitants to produce a surplus of rice and other grains, which they could then trade to less productive communities. Thus, Graham Connah concluded in *African Civilizations* that "it seems most likely that an extensive trading network existed within West Africa before the Arab trade across the Sahara was developed. The savanna towns were indeed 'ports' at the edge of the 'sea of land' . . . but they were ports with a vast trading hinterland that was already developed. After all, what ship would ever visit a port unless there was a chance of a cargo to collect?" Archaeologists' findings confirm once again that no one group or culture was responsible for the success of West Africa; the region's growth was the result of the rich ferment of many different traditions.

That ferment had long before shown its tendency to tear down the very empires it had helped build up. Less than 40 years after the death of Askia Muhammad, his careful work began to come undone. During the reign of Askia Muhammad II (1582–86), the Hausa states in the east rose up against the rule of

The great emperor Askia Muhammad was buried in this tomb at Gao, the seat of the Songhay government.

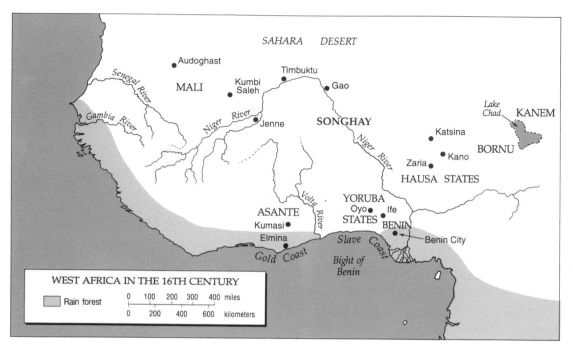

WEST AFRICA IN THE 16TH CENTURY

Rain forest

0   100   200   300   400 miles

0   200   400   600   kilometers

From the 1460s to the end of the next century, Songhay's rulers dominated the Western Sudan. This map indicates both the breadth of their empire and the diversity of their West African rivals.

Songhay, and the Moroccans of North Africa seized the salt deposits at Teghaza, in the northern reaches of the empire. The latter event led to a full-scale war between Morocco and Songhay.

The Moroccans were a formidable enemy. In 1578, they had successfully defended their territory against an invading force from the European nation of Portugal, annihilating the Portuguese king Sebastian and almost 25,000 of his soldiers at the Battle of Alcazarquivir. (By this victory, they delayed the European penetration of Africa by more than two centuries.) Then, in 1590, Morocco's sultan Mulay Ahmad, known as Mulay the Victorious, sent a 4,600-man army south through the Sahara to capture the riches of Songhay. Such a small force should not have stood much chance against the armies of Songhay, but the Moroccans had two important factors weighing in their favor. First, at least half of them were equipped with harquebuses. The harquebus, a European invention, was an early form of musket, and as such provided its users with a tremendous advantage over opponents armed with swords, spears, and bows and arrows. Second, many of the Moroccan troops were Spanish and Portuguese Christians who had been taken prisoner in warfare or captured by Muslim pirates. Their lives had been spared on condition that they become Muslims and fight for the sultan. Though they had no personal loyalty to Mulay, they certainly knew that retreat would mean either death in the Sahara or execution when they returned to Morocco, and they fought with the ferocity of desperate men.

The first battle between Morocco and Songhay, which took place at Tondibi in March 1591, resulted in a clear-cut victory for the invaders. Fighting their way steadily southward, they penetrated both Gao and Timbuktu and carried off much gold and other valuable goods. The armies of Songhay's Ishaq II proved incapable of driving the Moroccans back across the desert, but the country people did what they could to harass the invaders. The scholar al-Sa'di provided a vivid account of the chaos caused by the Moroccans: "This expeditionary force found the Sudan one of God's most favored countries in prosperity, comfort, security, and vitality. . . . Then all that changed; security gave place to danger, prosperity made way for misery and calamity, whilst affliction and distress succeeded well being. Over the length and breadth of the land people began to devour one another, raids and war spared neither life nor wealth. Disorder spread and intensified until it became universal."

As the disorder prevented the towns from providing riches to the crown and the empire of Songhay lost its splendid possessions, the country people—the true foundation of Songhay's power—once again became the backbone of the nation. In the rise and fall of Songhay, history seemed to have come full circle.

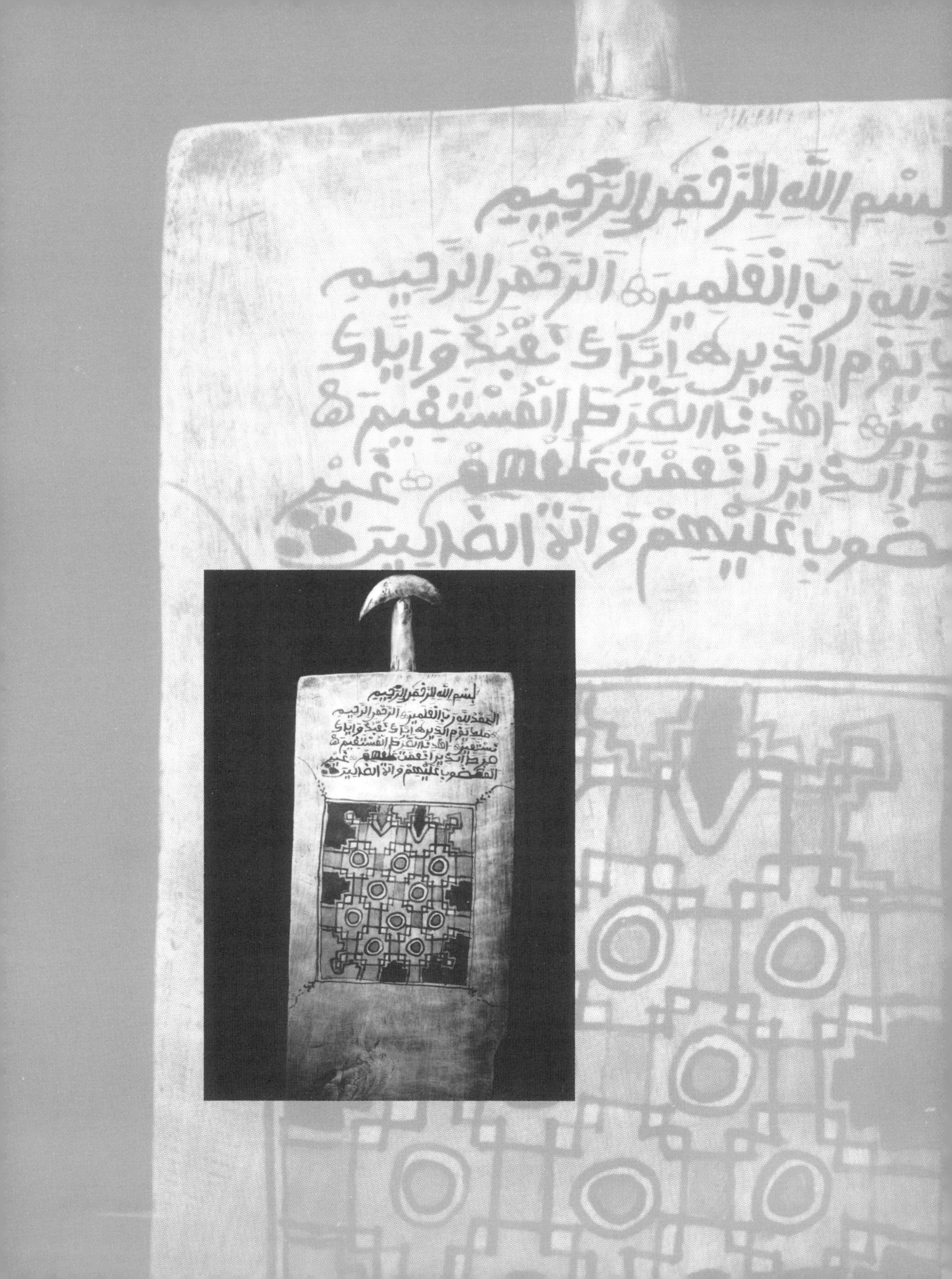
بسم الله الرحمن الرحيم

5

THE LAKE PEOPLE

I N the entire western Sudan, there is only one
sizable body of water—Lake Chad. The lake, which
can cover an area as large as 9,000 square miles in
periods of adequate rainfall, is situated on the border
of the present-day nations of Chad, Niger, and Nigeria. As early as the beginning of the Iron Age, Lake
Chad was a natural point of settlement along the trade
routes leading into West Africa, both from the Sahara
and from Egypt. Thus the people who lived in the
region were in touch with much of the rest of Africa.

Around 850, the Kanuri people founded the state
of Kanem in the vicinity of Lake Chad. The exact
origin of the Kanuri is unknown, but there is reason
to believe that they were made up in part of migrants
from the Nile valley who brought a somewhat different racial and cultural strain into the Sudan. These
migrants, known as the Sao, no longer exist as a
distinct people, but archaeologists have uncovered
intriguing evidence of their civilization. "With the

*This wooden board from Hausaland, in what is now northern
Nigeria, is inscribed with Arabic text from the Koran. Such
boards were used as writing tablets in the region's Islamic schools.*

A 19th-century engraving shows cattle visiting a watering hole near Lake Chad, the largest body of water in the western Sudan. The roofs of a village can be seen in the background.

appearance of the Sao in the neighborhood of Lake Chad," Basil Davidson has written, "there is both an end to the civilizing trail which had led from the valley of the Nile and the beginning of another civilization. For the Sao constructed towns, fashioned rams' heads in pottery, worked in bronze . . . , elevated women to influence in government, and generally elaborated a mode of life that was plainly a new synthesis of the African east and African west."

The Kanuris' new state was governed by kings belonging to the Sefawa dynasty, and by the 12th century, these kings eventually followed many of their fellow rulers in adopting Islam. The act of reaching out to the Muslim trading powers of the north and east remained an almost certain formula for prosperity, expansion, and influence.

By the reign of Dunama Dibbelimi (1221–59), the state of Kanem had grown into an empire. Kanem's original boundaries had expanded around Lake Chad and hundreds of miles to the north, absorbing trade routes that extended to the borders of North Africa. Kanem maintained this position for more than a century, until it came under assault from the Bulala, a neighboring people to the east. By the end of the 14th century, Kanem had lost its territory east of the lake, including its capital city, Nkimi. The reigning Sefawa king, Umar, then established a new capital at Bornu. For this reason, the Sefawa empire has usually been known to historians as Kanem-Bornu.

Having retreated at first, the rulers of Kanem-Bornu gathered their strength and resumed the offensive. During the 15th century, Kanem-Bornu regained many of its former possessions and also made major inroads to the west, in the territory of the Hausa people. However, the greatest era of the empire did not begin until the reign of Idris Alooma, which extended from 1580 until 1617 (some historians have suggested the alternate dates of 1571–1603).

Like Askia Muhammad of Songhay and other previous empire builders, Idris believed that the future of his people lay in the path of Islam. He took measures to promote the influence of Islamic law, even going so far as to submit his own affairs to the judgment of the Muslim qadis.

Idris Alooma led Kanem-Bornu to its highest level of influence. By the time he was done, his empire extended far beyond the boundaries of the original Kanem: it reached all the way to Murzuk in the northern Sahara and far beyond Lake Chad to the hills of Darfur in the east. As the ruler of this domain, Idris was so powerful that he received ambassadors from the Ottoman Empire, which had spread from Turkey throughout the Middle East and was then in control of Cairo, Egypt. Idris's rule roughly coincided with that of England's Elizabeth I; though much less has been written about him, he was no less successful or grand a monarch.

In addition to the king, Kanem-Bornu was run by a council of governors, perhaps a dozen in number. The governors were all members of the ruling Sefawa family, and each of them presided over a province of the empire. Because of the rebelliousness of neighboring peoples, especially those in the east, the borders of Kanem-Bornu were constantly shifting. But the king and the governors were able to maintain enough stability that trade went on without serious disruption. From the north and east came Arabian horses, fine metalware, salt, and copper; from Kanem-Bornu, kola nuts, gold, and ivory reached the outside world.

After the death of Idris, peace and prosperity reigned for another century—under the kings Muhammad, Ibrahim, and Omar—even though much of the Sudan was in turmoil because of the decline of Mali and Songhay. The tide of history did not even begin to overtake Kanem-Bornu until the end of the 17th century, when raiders from both north and south pressed in on the empire. The Sefawa carried on despite their shrinking borders. The last representative of their line, Ahmad, held the throne until 1846, when he was ousted by the Fulani leader Uthman Dan Fodio. Thus the Sefawa had enjoyed an unbroken reign from the 9th century into the 19th, a record of stability and prosperity rarely equaled in human history.

Throughout its history, Kanem-Bornu had been in close contact—sometimes peaceful, sometimes violent—with the Hausa states, located directly west of Kanem in what is now northern Nigeria. The main Hausa states—Biram, Daura, Gobir, Kano, Katsina, Rano, and Zaria—had a royal tradition nearly as old as Kanem's, and in many ways they resembled the fiefs of medieval Europe. Each of the Hausa states was ruled by its own king, and for as long as they had existed they had competed with one another for wealth and power in the region. The life of each centered on a fortified city in which the people of the countryside would take shelter in times of war or other crises. As in Europe, the country people paid a tax to the local leader (*sarki*) in the form of goods or money. The sarkis were subservient to the king, to whom they paid a tax of their own. In addition to offering protection, the cities provided markets for the produce of the countryside and served as an outlet for visiting traders.

Much current knowledge about the Hausa states derives from the *Kano Chronicle*, a collection of oral accounts that were written down long after the events they described. The chronicle makes it clear that the Hausa kings faced the same challenge as other West African rulers: they had to balance the political and religious needs of the cities against those of the countryside. For example, the chronicle relates that a 13th-century sarki named Shekkaru was advised by his counselors to send troops to fight against country people who were showing signs of disloyalty. The counselors argued, as many have before and since, that if Shekkaru tried to negotiate with the people, they would consider him weak. Shekkaru, however, believed that bloodshed should always be a last resort. (Fighting, after all, disrupted trade.) He received a delegation of rural chiefs who were also eager to avoid a violent clash. "If the lands of a ruler are wide, he should be patient," they told the sarki. "But if his lands are not wide, he will certainly not be able to gain

This offering bowl, a product of the Yoruba tribe, was made to hold kola nuts—bitter, caffeine-containing seeds valued throughout West Africa for their stimulant properties.

possession of the whole countryside by impatience." Shekkaru understood the wisdom of their words and decided to work with them rather than try to conquer them.

As the centuries unfolded, none of the Hausa kings was able to acquire truly "wide lands" by bringing all of the Hausa states under his rule. On the whole, the Hausa cooperated more than they fought, largely because they had an important role in the economy of West Africa. Situated closer than any other savanna state to the Niger delta and the forestlands of the coast, the Hausa states were in close contact with the Yoruba people, who harvested kola nuts (valued for their stimulant properties); in turn, the Yoruba could only get the outside goods they needed through Hausaland.

As a result of this trade, the Hausa cities grew to be as prosperous and cultured as any in the Sudan. They were protected by soldiers whose elaborate suits of armor were famous for their strength and splendor. Leo Africanus, traveling in the area during the 17th century, noted the wealth of the rulers and the size of their armies and was especially impressed by the state of Kano, which was rich in corn, rice, and cotton: "Also here are many deserts and wild, woody mountains containing many springs of water. In these woods grow plenty of wild citrons and lemons, which differ not much in taste from the best of all. In the midst of this province stands a town of the same name, the walls and houses whereof are built for the most part of a kind of chalk [the typical clay of West Africa]. The inhabitants are rich merchants and most civil people."

Prosperity had its price. Taxes in the Hausa states were high, and Leo Africanus also noted on his travels that people outside the cities lived poorly: during the winter, they had nothing but animal skins to cover themselves with, and during the summer, they went all but naked. The Hausa kings had also developed an extensive system of slave labor. The slaves were obtained from neighboring states during military raids. Abdullah Burja, a 15th-century ruler of Kano, was said to command more than 20,000 slaves in a number of settlements. Some of these slaves were recruited into full-time armies; the military establishments originated by Askia Muhammad of Songhay were now common throughout the Sudan.

In addition to the burden they imposed on the countryside, the Hausa cities were wealthy enough to be seen as a rich prize by potential conquerors.

("It is the hen with chickens that fears the hawk," runs a Hausa proverb.) Askia Muhammad himself conquered Kano during the 16th century and compelled its ruler to pay him one-third of the city's revenue. Following Kano's submission, Zaria became the strongest of the Hausa states. Zaria is noteworthy because its rise was due in large part to the efforts of female rulers, Barkwa Turunda and her daughter, Queen Amina, who conquered a number of neighboring states and undertook many building projects in their domains. Eventually, the states subdued by Zaria, notably Jukun, turned the tables on their conquerors

Traders enter the city of Kano, Nigeria, one of the most prosperous Hausa centers of commerce.

and enjoyed their own periods of dominance. But the wars between the rival states do not appear to have been especially long or destructive, because the general prosperity of Hausaland continued. In fact, the 16th century represented a peak of achievement for Hausaland and for neighboring areas of the Sudan.

Like many of the nations of Europe, West Africans were by this time moving away from a long-held idea: that the king was not a high-ranking public figure, but a higher form of being. According to Nehemiah Levtzion, this idea may have reached its absolute peak in Kanem in earlier times; in his discussion of the subject, he quotes the testimony of al-Muhallabi, a Muslim scholar who visited Kanem during the 10th century: "They exalt their king and worship him instead of God. They imagine that he does not eat. . . . If any of his subjects meet the camels which carry the food [secretly to his palace] he is instantly killed. . . . Their religion is the worship of their kings, for they believe that they bring life and death, sickness and health."

In the place of divine kingship, West Africans gradually developed the idea of constitutional monarchy, in which the king's power was limited by carefully drawn political rules. By the 18th century, the Hausa kings were able to take action on important issues only with the consent of senior advisers. In addition to counselors who were heads of major descent lines, the rulers also surrounded themselves with individuals known as king's men. Many of the king's men were eunuchs, men who had been castrated so that

they could not begin descent lines of their own;
thus their only loyalty would be to the king. In
many cases, the king's men came into conflict
with the advisers who had been appointed because of their birth; when this happened, skillful
rulers could play off one faction against another
and gain leverage in making decisions.

Even though they achieved a high level of political
development, the Hausa states never combined to
form a powerful empire, even after the decline of
Kanem-Bornu. The Hausa kings were simply unable
to abandon their rivalries, and they wasted much
energy and valuable resources in fighting one another.
By the mid-18th century, the westernmost states were
repeatedly ravaged by Tuareg raiders from the Sahara.
And by the beginning of the following century, the
Hausa kings faced a full-scale revolt from within—far
more dangerous than any external threat.

The rebellion was not a simple grab for power but
rather a reform movement within the Islamic community, to which all the rulers belonged. The movement
arose among the Fulani, who had played an important
role throughout the history of the Sudan, and it was
led by Uthman Dan Fodio. Though he was a member
of the Quadiriyya, a Muslim brotherhood that was
soon to be considered conservative, Uthman adopted
a radical stance. He denounced the luxury of the
Hausa cities and called for substantial reforms in the
way the states were governed. His message was designed to rally the support of the humble country
people, Muslim and non-Muslim alike, who readily
agreed with Uthman's words condemning "the col-
lecting of concubines and fine clothes and horses that
run in the towns, not on the battlefields, and the
devouring of gifts of influence, booty, and bribery."

Uthman and his followers deposed the Hausa
kings one by one. But they did not find it easy to

achieve their cherished goal of the ideal Islamic state
that would carry out all the dictates of the Koran.
Disputes arose among the Fulani leaders, and these
were not resolved until Sultan Muhammad Bello,
Uthman's son, imposed his will upon the Fulani by
force of arms. By that measure, however, the democratic element of the reform movement was destroyed.
Thus the Hausa states finally achieved unity under
Muhammad Bello, but they also lost the political
qualities that had made them unique. By the early
20th century, the Hausa had a new set of masters, the
colonial governors of the British Empire, who also
took control of the former territory of Kanem-Bornu
around Lake Chad. Today, the Islamic culture that
blossomed in these regions survives in the northern
part of Nigeria, Africa's most populous republic.

6

THE FORESTLANDS

T HE doom and ironwood trees were frequent; the path was a labyrinth of the most capricious windings, the roots of the cotton trees obstructing it continually, and our progress was generally by stepping and jumping up and down, rather than walking. . . . Immense trunks of fallen trees presented constant barriers to our progress, and increased our fatigues from the labor of scaling them. . . . The large trees were covered with parasites and convulvuli, and the climbing plants, like small cables, ascending the trunks to some height, abruptly shot downwards, crossed to the opposite trees, and threaded each other in such a perplexity of twists and turnings, that it soon became impossible to trace them in the general entanglement." Such was the experience of a 19th-century European, quoted by Graham Connah, in the tropical rain forest of the West African coast. Protected since the Stone Age by this dense and forbidding landscape, the peoples of the forest enjoyed a way of life strikingly different from that of the inhabitants of the savanna.

Between the 10th and 16th centuries, Yoruba artists in the city of Ife created bronze and terra-cotta portraits of exceptional strength and beauty. The elegance of this bronze cast is characteristic of the Ife legacy.

A man from the modern state of Guinea crosses a narrow bridge in the West African rain forest.

The Igbo, for example, who occupied a large area just east of the Niger River, had neither kings nor chiefs. Living in forest villages and skilled in farming, they practiced what is known as segmentary government. The basis of segmentary government is the family unit. As a family grows and new generations begin their own branches, new segments break off from the original line and form a distinct unit in a nearby area.

At first glance, this way of life might appear to cause disunity and weakness. However, the Igbo religion included many ceremonies designed to strengthen family and community ties. Some of these ceremonies emphasized the importance of a family's common ancestors; others formally transferred power from older segments of a family to newer segments, thus reminding all parties of their rights and responsibilities.

Throughout Igboland, different groups developed their own responses to situations calling for mutual aid. Some groups, such as the Ama and Ozo, formed associations that were governed by the wealthiest members; others, such as the Tallensi, insisted on strict equality in decision making. Compared to the centralized states and empires of the savanna, with their elaborate rituals of kingship and luxurious royal courts, the Igbo maintained a remarkably democratic way of life that was much closer in spirit to the 19th and 20th centuries than to the Middle Ages.

A neighboring people who enjoyed an equally distinctive way of life was the Yoruba. Living to the west of the Niger, the Yoruba traced their roots to the very dawn of civilization. According to one of their traditions, both the Yoruba nation and humanity itself were created at the town of Ile-Ife.

In one version of the Yoruba creation story, the world was created by the Supreme Being, Olodumare, through his agent Orishanla, who then brought human beings out of the sky to dwell on the earth. But according to a parallel belief, the world was created by the god Odududwa, who came not from the sky but from the east: he brought the Yoruba with him to the land of the Niger and then sired rulers for various communities. As Basil Davidson has interpreted the two traditions, they do not really conflict but rather supplement one another: "What right could any peo-

The Igbo religion, like many other African faiths, involved many practices that strengthened family and community ties. This female figure comes from an Igbo shrine devoted to family ancestors.

ple have to come from somewhere else and settle in a new land? . . . To seal their right to occupy and settle, incomers must make their peace with the Spirit of the Earth. They could do this only through a process of spiritual reconciliation sanctioned by appropriate rites. Otherwise the Spirit of the Earth would not recognize their legitimate existence in the land."

Archaeologists have confirmed that the ancestors of the Yoruba came to the West African forestland from the central Sudan (not the east, as the tradition claims) sometime after A.D. 700, blending with peoples who had occupied the Niger region since the Stone Age. The older inhabitants were already skilled in iron making and may have been related to the brilliantly creative Nok culture. The newcomers, though less adept as craftspeople, brought a new level of political sophistication.

Because of this influx of political ideas, the new Yoruba communities developed quite differently from those of the Igbo. Though the Yoruba practiced the same farming techniques in the dense forests, they did not limit the size of their settlements as the Igbo did. The Yoruba built a number of large towns, most of which were surrounded by sizable walls. Each town was ruled by an *oba*, who was said to be descended from Odududwa, the god who had brought the Yoruba into the forestland.

Yoruba towns did resemble Igbo villages in their general structure: they were organized on segmentary lines, with each family group occupying its own distinct area. All the dwellings belonging to a family were clustered together in a compound known as an *agbo'le*. At the center of this compound was the house of the head of the descent line to which all the various offshoots belonged. Following the same idea, the agbo'les were clustered around the house of the oba, which stood in the center of the town.

The oba was generally chosen by a council of

The tradition that produced this terra-cotta head from Ife drew inspiration from the Nok culture, a civilization that may have preceded the Yoruba empire by as much as a thousand years.

chiefs. But when major decisions had to be made, the Yoruba did not practice the village democracy of the Igbo. On the contrary, the oba alone held the power to take action, aided by his personal servants and messengers, who formed a class comparable to the officialdom of the savanna kingdoms. For truly large-scale decision making, the various obas and their

This richly ornamented Ife half-figure is believed to represent an oni, *the highest authority in the Ebi system of government.*

towns were linked through the Yoruba's Ebi system of government. In the Ebi system, each town had the status of a descent line: all were united as equals in the great "family" of the Yoruba people, under the guidance of a supreme authority, the *oni* of Ife.

Ife reached its peak during the 14th century. As a

civilization, it is remembered not so much for its political majesty as for the brilliance of its craftspeople and artists. Beginning as early as the 10th century, its sculptors and metalworkers produced works of art that were a direct outgrowth of the Nok culture. Fashioned both in terra-cotta and in bronze, the sculptures are predominantly portrayals of human heads. Their combination of realistic detail, abstract design, and spiritual intensity places them among the world's greatest works of art. Indeed, the rest of the world spent many centuries catching up with Ife: many of the pioneers of modern art in Europe, such as the great Spanish painter Pablo Picasso, acknowledged the influence of African art on their seemingly revolutionary works.

Ife's accomplishments ensured that it would remain the spiritual center of the Yoruba nation. But by the 16th century, Ife and all the other Yoruba communities were gradually overshadowed by the town of Oyo. Situated in the northern part of the forest belt, Oyo—one of the newer towns—was in an ideal position to benefit from trading opportunities with the savanna states.

Before it could truly take the lead in Yorubaland, Oyo had to solve the problem of self-defense. Throughout its history, the town had been victimized by two of the Hausa states, Nupe and Borgu, both of which possessed powerful mounted armies. Oyo's *alafin* (king) Orompoto resolved to build up his forces to match those of his enemies, but to do so he had to overcome a serious obstacle. Oyo was situated in a region inhabited by the tsetse fly, one of Africa's most dangerous pests. The bloodsucking tsetse not only threatens humans with a variety of diseases, such as sleeping sickness; it also transmits a fatal ailment, known as nagana, to cattle and horses. For this reason, it was impossible for the people of Oyo to breed their own horses. But under Orompoto they discovered that horses imported from North Africa could survive the tsetse long enough to be serviceable. Fortunately, the people of Oyo were wealthy enough to purchase a steady supply of mounts from the north. Orompoto trained a crack force of 1,000 cavalry, and Oyo no longer had any problems with its neighbors.

Its security assured, Oyo set about building an empire. In addition to its favorable geographic position, Oyo had much to offer traders. The Yoruba excelled in the art of making fine cotton goods, and their textiles were in great demand throughout Africa, Asia, and Europe. They continued to produce world-class metalwork, as well as first-rate bowls and jugs. The more income these products brought them, the better the Yoruba were able to maintain their formidable cavalry.

From the 16th through the 18th centuries, the combination of commercial and military power allowed Oyo to spread its influence both into the savanna and deeper into the forestlands. Oyo's most important conquest was the state of Dahomey: this acquisition placed Oyo in control of a seaport, Porto-Novo on the Gulf of Guinea, from which the Yoruba were able to deal with the European merchants now plying the coast. As they became ever more powerful as traders and warriors, the alafins of Oyo assumed almost superhuman dimensions in the eyes of their subjects. According to Basil Davidson, the people of Dahomey told an English visitor "that when the Oyo people want to go to war, their general 'spreads the hide of a buffalo before the door of his tent and pitches a spear in the ground on each side of it. Between these spears the soldiers march until the multitude which pass over the hide have worn a hole in it. As soon as this happens, the general presumes that his forces are numerous enough to take the field.'"

By the end of the 18th century, Oyo was said to control as many as 6,600 towns and villages. However, the alafins became so intent on trading that they began to neglect their army, which was ultimately the basis of their power in the region. In addition, their method of rule was ill-suited to the task of governing a large empire. In theory, Oyo had a perfectly workable method of controlling conquered territories: a Yoruba chief lived in the capital city of each subject state and ran its affairs, much in the manner of the European colonial governors who were later to make their appearance in Africa. As the empire grew, however, the alafins of Oyo found it increasingly difficult to keep in touch with their governors. The difficulty sprang from the very nature of their society. Like most of the forest peoples, the Yoruba had never deviated in any way from their ancestral religions; even the rulers had not felt the need to curry favor with Muslim traders by converting to Islam. The old ways satisfied all the Yoruba's social, spiritual, and artistic needs but did not provide them with one tool that had proved highly useful to the rulers of the Sudan: the art of reading and writing.

As their society grew, the Yoruba had clearly not been hampered by their lack of literacy. Indeed, if they had developed a literary tradition, they might never have felt the need to express themselves in the magnificent art of Ife. But once Oyo moved away from the Ebi style of family-oriented government and began to emulate the far-flung empires of the savanna, the illiteracy of alafins and governors became a severe handicap. The alafins could not issue any written instructions to their public servants. They had to rely on their messengers to memorize verbal commands and deliver them accurately after traveling long distances: the potential for mistakes and treachery in this method was clearly unlimited.

Subject states and rivals were eager to assert themselves against the power of the alafins, and they watched them for signs of weakness. The situation was

The rulers of Oyo never converted to Islam but remained true to the traditional religions of the African forestlands. Oyo leaders used this brass rattle to call on ancestral spirits.

further complicated by tensions within the Yoruba community, as the nobles of other towns often resented Oyo's departure from the Ebi tradition of equality. In addition, Oyo's increasing trade in slaves and firearms was creating unstable conditions along the coast.

Before long, the smaller states on the coast took advantage of Oyo's state of confusion and tried to seize control of the trade routes in their territory, disrupting Oyo's economy. Roland Oliver and Anthony Atmore have recounted the course of events in *Africa Since 1800*:

> The beginning of the end came in 1817, when the great chiefs of Oyo, led by Alfonja of Ilorin, sent an empty calabash [a gourd used as a bottle or dipper] to the *alafin* (king) Aole, thus signifying that they no longer recognized his authority. Aole accepted the hint in traditional fashion by committing suicide, but not before he had uttered his famous curse. From the palace forecourt he shot three arrows, one to the north, one to the south, and one to the west, saying, "My curse be on you for your disloyalty and disobedience, so let your children disobey you. If you send them on an errand, let them never return to bring you word again. To all the points I shot my arrows will you be carried as slaves. My curse will carry you to the sea and beyond the seas, slaves will rule over you, and you, their masters, will become slaves."

Forming another threat from the coast, the people of Dahomey were growing strong enough to cause problems for Oyo's military forces. And the Fulani, who had taken control of the Hausa states, began to expand under the rule of Muhammad Bello, swooping down on the northern Oyo towns. By about 1840, the power of Oyo had been broken for all time.

Oyo may have vanished into the mists of history, but the civilization of the Yoruba lived on through the trials of slavery and colonialism. Today, the 10 million Yoruba of Nigeria form the nation's third-largest ethnic group. As the Yoruba continue to practice their traditional occupations, such as farming and cotton weaving, their ancient city-dwelling traditions remain intact: Nigeria's 10 largest cities are predominantly Yoruba. Moreover, Olodumare and the other Yoruba gods are powerfully alive, not only in Africa but also in the Americas—particularly in Brazil and Cuba— where many Yoruba were transported as slaves during the 18th and 19th centuries. The harmony and depth of the Yoruba worldview has exerted widespread appeal even among non-Africans, and the ancient art inspired by these beliefs remains one of the treasures of world culture.

7

GRANDEUR IN THE DELTA

WHILE the Yoruba were developing their network of great towns in the forestland, another ancient people, the Edo, were establishing themselves in the Niger delta, the region where the great river forms several branches before it flows into the Gulf of Guinea. The Edo's traditions show that they were in close contact with the Yoruba: they trace the beginnings of what was to become the powerful empire of Benin to Prince Oranmiyan, a son of the Yoruba god Odududwa.

Despite this time-honored connection, neither the Edo nor Benin was ever dominated by the Yoruba states. The Edo's position in the Niger delta, along the main travel route between the sea and the inland regions, gave them rich opportunities for trade. By the 14th century, Benin was a rising commercial power; by the 15th century, it was a mighty empire. Ewuare, the Edo *oba* (king) who led the way to expansion, ascended the throne around 1440. Ewuare is credited

This 17th-century bronze plaque from Benin depicts members of the oba's *court. The figure on the left is holding a sistrum—a kind of rattle used by the musicians of the ancient Near East.*

85

by Edo tradition with conquering more than 200 towns and villages and with developing Benin City, which became the capital of the empire.

A century or so later, a Dutch traveler named Olfert Dapper found the city highly impressive:

> At the gate where I went in on horseback, I saw a very big wall, very thick and made of earth, with a very deep and broad ditch outside it. . . . Inside the gate, and along the great street just mentioned, you see many other great streets on either side, and these are also straight and do not bend. . . . The houses in this town stand in good order, each one close and evenly placed with its neighbor, just as the houses in Holland stand. . . . The king's court is very great. It is built around many square-shaped yards. These yards have surrounding galleries where sentries are always placed. I myself went into the court far enough to pass through four great yards like this, and yet wherever I looked I could still see gate after gate which opened into other yards.

Oba Ewuare and his 16th-century successor Oba Esigie were equally famed for their innovations in government. Ewuare founded the State Council of Benin to govern the growing empire, and Esigie developed a civil service, recruiting officials on the basis of ability rather than social position.

Laying the ground for the later history of West Africa, these kings developed large-scale trade relations with Europeans. By the 15th and 16th centuries, Europe had recovered from the ravages of war and plague and was entering an era of expansion. At the forefront of the expansionist movement was the nation of Portugal, situated on the Atlantic coast of the Iberian Peninsula. Portugal, a narrow kingdom with a long coastline, became a nation of seafarers, and Portuguese ships had been sailing to North Africa since the beginning of the 14th century. However, Portuguese sailors were for many years unable to pass beyond Cape Bojador in the northwest because of the

This richly detailed Benin sculpture represents a Portuguese soldier brandishing a matchlock. Arriving in Benin in 1472, the Portuguese left a deep impression on the lives of the Edo, giving them direct access to European weapons and other manufactured goods.

prevailing north-to-south winds: a ship that sailed down the western coast of Africa could not return. With the invention of the lateen (triangular) sail and the sternpost rudder, however, ships could finally sail into the wind; and when the Portuguese added these features to the newly designed caravel, a smaller and more maneuverable ship, they had nothing to fear from the winds south of Bojador. In 1472, Portuguese sailors dropped anchor in the Bight of Benin, a wide bay in the Gulf of Guinea, and made contact with the wealthy rulers of the Edo's growing empire.

At first, relations between the two continents benefited both Europeans and Africans. The Africans were able to purchase manufactured goods and metals such as copper from the Europeans instead of sending all the way to North Africa; they were also able to sell their gold, ivory, and spices directly to the Europeans without the use of middlemen. As a result of their contact with Europeans, the rulers of Benin adopted arts and interests that were not usually found in the forest belt. Oba Esigie, who came to power in 1504 and reigned for nearly 50 years, was said, for example, to be able both to speak and to read Portuguese. He also became adept in the art of astrology, the study of the influence of the stars and planets upon human affairs.

During Esigie's reign, English ships made their first contact with Benin, landing at the river port of Gwato, and the British were soon followed by their Dutch rivals. Esigie quickly established a monopoly on the new source of trade. According to one Dutch traveler, "Nobody is allowed to buy anything from the Europeans on this coast, except the agents and merchants whom the king has named for this purpose. As soon as one of our ships drops anchor, the people inform the king, and the king appoints two or three agents and thirty or forty merchants whom he empowers to deal with the Europeans."

In the ensuing decades, however, the commerce between Europeans and West Africans took a more sinister turn. The change was brought about by the European conquest of the New World. As the European nations—Spain in particular—developed sizable

Heads of Portuguese traders surmount this ornamental ivory mask, made to be worn at the waist of an oba's costume.

colonies in the Americas, they created farming and mining operations that called for vast amounts of human labor. This demand could be met neither by the home countries nor by the native Indian populations of the Americas. The home countries were too small, and the Indians were unaccustomed to the kind of work required by their conquerors; when forced into it, they simply sickened and died. West Africans, on the other hand, were strong and hardy, and they had a long history of tropical farming and metal mining. Determined to make their New World enterprises profitable, the Europeans decided to solve their problem by importing labor from West Africa.

West Africa itself had no tradition of paid labor. Those Africans who did not live independently as farmers were usually organized into various forms of forced labor by African rulers. The wealth of the great empires had always rested upon the exploitation of the weak by the strong, an experience hardly limited to Africa. The Roman Empire; the great civilizations of Egypt, Persia, and Babylon; the Muslim caliphates of the Middle East and North Africa—all had taken slavery as a matter of course. Empires were built and solidified in no small part by the conquest of neighboring nations; as a result of those conquests, subject peoples were obliged—in addition to military service—to produce wealth for their new masters. All the great African leaders, from Mansa Musa to Askia Muhammad, had commanded vast numbers of slaves in their far-flung dominions as well as in their personal entourages. Europeans themselves had continued to enslave each other even as they entered the supposedly enlightened period known as the Renaissance; Italy's Venetian Republic, for example, did a brisk business during the 15th and 16th centuries by exporting Christian slaves from Europe to Muslim North Africa.

Because slavery was already a fact of life in West Africa, it was natural that a small-scale traffic in slaves began as soon as commercial contact was established with Europeans. In the beginning, the Portuguese

were willing to accept a certain number of slaves in exchange for their manufactured goods. But as the demand for slaves in the Americas exploded during the 17th century, the trade in human beings began to dominate the commercial relations between Europe and West Africa. At this point, West African rulers were increasingly in need of European firearms in order to maintain their power. The only way they could obtain these weapons was to provide large numbers of captives for the slave ships. Before long, rulers were going to war against their neighbors not to expand their territory but simply to take prisoners who could then be sold to the Europeans. In order to fight

Elmina Castle, built by the Portuguese in what is now Ghana, became the center of Dutch slave-trading activities in 1637. Pictured here is a courtyard of the female slave quarters, where women captured by the armies of West African rulers awaited shipment to the Americas.

This Igbo dance headdress shows a slave trader bringing a captive woman into European headquarters along the West African coast. By the 18th century, the slave trade had become one of the area's main industries.

these wars, they needed more firearms. And in order to obtain more firearms, they needed to supply more slaves. Thus West Africa was plunged into a vicious cycle that caused untold suffering and ultimately benefited no one but the slave traders.

The transatlantic slave trade not only corrupted the political life of West Africa; it also added a new level of injustice to the institution of slavery as Africans had known it. As Basil Davidson has pointed out, slaves in West African society had a far different position from those sent abroad: "These 'wageless workers' . . . were seldom or never mere chattels, persons without rights or hope of emancipation. . . . They were not . . . outcasts in the body politic. On the contrary, they were integral members of their community. Household slaves lived with their masters, often as members of the family. They could work themselves free of their obligations. They could marry their masters' daughters. They could become traders, leading men in peace and war, governors or sometimes even kings." No such possibilities lay in wait for Africans shipped to the Americas, where they suffered both the hardships of forced labor in a strange land and the added injury of being despised because of their race.

Though historians do not agree on the degree to which the massive slave trade disrupted the economic development of Africa, the effects were certainly significant. A number of areas were quickly depopulated of strong, hardworking men and women who produced both food and such handicrafts as the fine cottons for which Africa had been famous. Though the population in these regions eventually returned to its previous levels, the economy of West Africa suffered long-term damage. Africans who had once exported goods now had to import them, and the price of those imports was tallied in human lives.

The slave trade also upset the age-old political balance of West Africa. Subject peoples could no longer expect, in the natural course of events, to turn the tables on their conquerors and eventually begin their own empires. In the rising tide of violence and exploitation, which even the most enlightened rulers could not escape, Africans became more and more dependent on Europeans for their well-being and their political survival.

Benin was one of the states that suffered most from this corruption of the West African way of life. The inhabitants of Benin City continued to impress Europeans with their elegant dress and manners, but as the slave trade gained momentum, the obas began to lose their power. Firearms spread throughout the region at an uncontrollable pace, and the more these weapons got into the hands of Benin's rivals, the more chance there was of rebellion and attack by competing powers. Increasingly, the governors of outlying areas asserted their own power in defiance of the obas. Benin's empire shrank steadily in power and prestige until it was overwhelmed by British forces in 1897. All that remains of the great delta empire today is Benin City itself, a community of 160,000 in southern Nigeria. (The modern-day nation of Benin, formerly the French colony of Dahomey, is completely distinct from the vanished realm of the obas.)

For all the wealth and influence of its great days, Benin is remembered most of all for its brilliant works of art. The Europeans who plundered Benin in the late 19th and early 20th centuries were astonished by the beauty of the bronze plaques they discovered in the royal palace. Having convinced themselves that the people they were conquering represented a lower form of civilization, the colonialists could not believe that such works had been produced by "savage" Africans. Basil Davidson describes this process of cultural blindness: "More [plaques] were found . . . by the German Africanist Leo Frobenius, who attributed them to the heritage of Atlantis, the 'lost continent.' Other Europeans . . . thought these works of art must be of classical Greek lineage; or perhaps the creation of some solitary European of long ago who had arrived in Benin and conceived, by amazing genius, these 'un-African' masterpieces. Others again thought they were obvious products of the European Renaissance."

Later work by impartial archaeologists established beyond any doubt that the works found in Benin were produced between the 14th and 17th centuries and were indeed purely African. Without question, Benin's art developed directly from the Yoruba art of Ife, with one essential difference: whereas the Yoruba sculptors had worked in both terra-cotta and bronze, Benin's royal sculptors worked exclusively in bronze, an alloy of copper with tin and other metals. Humbler craftspeople often worked in other, locally available materials; among the great surviving works from Benin are a pair of carved ivory leopards whose spots are represented by inlaid bronze studs.

The shift to bronze occurred as copper became more readily available, first by way of North Africa and then through Portuguese traders. Benin's artists began by fashioning heads to adorn the altars of ancestors. As Benin became richer and grander, its sculptors began to create plaques to adorn the oba's palace. The plaques depicted a wide variety of subjects: obas with their vassals, religious rituals, musicians, birds, lizards, fish, and other images from nature. The art historian Jean Laude has written in *The Arts of Black Africa* that some degree of foreign influence may not, after all, have been entirely absent from the process of creation. "The forms of the plaques and the efforts of the artists to achieve a certain degree of perspective suggest that these works were inspired by engravings

The oba's palace in Benin City was adorned with bronze plaques portraying such diverse subjects as animals, musicians, soldiers, and figures of the royal court. In this fragment, a court musician beats a drum.

in illustrated European books which the artists had in their possession. But even if this hypothesis should be verified, it must be remembered that the pursuit of illusionistic effects and perspective is related to a psychological mode of apprehending the world and man: the concept of a stable and measurable space as the location of human activity or a spectacular setting for it. This concept is unique to Africa."

No one who looks at these works today can fail to perceive the qualities that set them apart from the art of any other culture—or doubt the splendor of the civilization that produced them.

8

UNDER THE KUMA TREE

IN the chaos following the decline of ancient Ghana around the beginning of the 13th century, many groups of farmers moved south to the forestlands in search of refuge. Among these groups were the Akan, who settled in the region around the Volta River, in what is now the nation of Ghana. In this new home the Akan soon discovered one of West Africa's largest goldfields, and as they grew more affluent through trade in the precious metal, they formed a number of small states based upon descent lines.

Sometime after 1600, a group of Akan farmers from the coastal town of Adansi moved northward in search of more land and a share of the gold trade. Settling near a small lake in the forestland, they built the state of Asantemanso. As this new trade center

This wooden doll, with its narrow body, long neck, and large, flattened head, is known as an akuaba. In Asante, pregnant women carried such figures to ensure easy childbirth and beautiful children.

grew in wealth, other groups from Adansi moved north to join their former townspeople, and the people of Asantemanso and the surrounding region came to call themselves the Asante.

Though they had succeeded in bettering their lot, the Asante were still not in the forefront of the Akan peoples. In fact, the nearby state of Denkyira controlled many of their activities, charging them heavy taxes and forcing them to produce a certain number of slaves each year. The Asante's only hope of real progress lay in uniting their various communities, but until around the close of the 17th century, this goal remained elusive. In the end, the key to Asante unity turned out to be religion—the same force that had formed the basis of so many social institutions in Africa.

An Asante king named Osei Tutu, who came to power around 1695, discovered a way to use his people's spiritual beliefs to draw them together. His approach centered on the Asante's traditional symbol of leadership: the *akonnua,* or royal stool. The most important element in the Asante's kingship ceremony was the moment when a new monarch took possession of the akonnua, swearing his fidelity to the people and pledging to serve all the Asante rather than his own particular descent line.

After he had completed this ceremony, Osei Tutu called an assembly of the Asante people. The various chiefs and representatives were addressed by Osei Tutu's ally, an *okomfo* (priest) named Anokye. Anokye produced another akonnua, this one partially covered in gold, and placed it on Osei Tutu's knees. The Golden Stool,

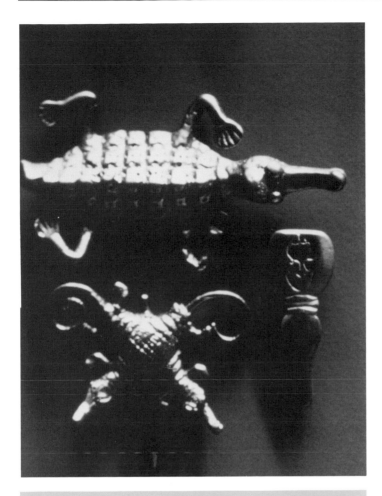

Asante traders used these decorative brass weights to measure gold dust.

Anokye told the people, had come down from the sky at the will of Nyame, the principal god of the Akan; it contained the soul of the Asante, and it was Nyame's desire that the Asante unite and become a great people. But they could only accomplish this by following the anointed guardian of the Golden Stool, Osei Tutu.

Osei Tutu had astutely called the assembly at a time when the Asante were under political and military pressure, and the people were prepared to accept the symbolic importance of the Golden Stool, to put aside their separate interests and work for the well-being of the nation. As soon as Osei Tutu had secured this promise, he took steps to ensure that the Asante union would not dissolve as quickly as past alliances. For example, he established a law that made it a crime for any of the Asante to speak about the history of his or her own group; instead, everyone had to speak of the Asante people as a whole. "'Ritual' and 'politics,' here as elsewhere, marched hand in hand," Basil Davidson wrote of this process. "Whether as the Golden Stool, the sacred spears of Central African kings, or the crown and sceptre of the monarchs of Europe, possession of the royal regalia provided the ultimate justification of political action. They were seen as the decisive instruments for transforming powers gained by superior force, intrigue, or good fortune into moral rights peculiar to the king."

Osei Tutu went on to rule the Asante until his death in 1717. He well understood that unity was meaningless without strength, and he immediately built up the Asante army by dividing it into four sections corresponding to the corners of a square: left, right, front, and rear. The head of an Asante state was appointed to command each section, and all the Asante warriors were assigned to one section or another on the basis of geography.

His army thus organized, Osei Tutu set out to defeat Denkyira in battle. For a time Bosianti, the king of Denkyira, was able to negotiate with Osei Tutu and forestall what he knew would be a costly war. He argued that the Asante and the people of Denkyira could do far better by cooperating than by fighting. Bosianti offered to release the Asante states from part of their obligation to provide gold and slaves. He also promised to help the Asante buy guns from the Dutch traders who were operating from the city of Elmina on the coast.

Though Osei Tutu did not really have faith in

Bosianti's offer of friendship, the conciliatory attitude of Denkyira kept him from going to war for many years. But when Bosianti was replaced by a new ruler who demanded heavier taxes from the Asante, Osei Tutu took the field. At first the Asante suffered heavy losses at the hands of the seasoned Denkyira forces, but in the end their efficient military organization carried the day. By 1701 they had subdued Denkyira's troops and gained control of much Denkyira territory. Among the possessions that fell into their hands was a trading contract with the Dutch. This document gave the Asante direct access to the Europeans, and its procurement was to have important consequences.

Before these consequences could unfold, the Asante confronted the task of empire building. Much of their territorial expansion was directed by Opoku Ware, who became king around 1720 and ruled for 30 years. His first challenge was to defeat a combined force of enemy states, including Denkyira, Sefwi, and Akwapim—a task he accomplished only after two bloody wars in which the Asante capital of Kumasi was temporarily captured. Opoku Ware went on to conquer a number of other neighboring states, such as Banda, Gonja, and Dagomba. By the late 1740s, Asante controlled the trade routes of the Middle Niger region.

During the second half of the 18th century and into the 19th century, Asante remained the supreme power in the region. Kings such as Osei Kwadwo (1764–77) added more territory through military conquest and made important reforms in government. Like other imperial peoples, the Asante found that they could not manage their complicated affairs through a handful of high-born administrators. Osei Kwadwo, therefore, began the practice of appointing outstanding individuals to important posts, regardless of their social station, and this program was followed by his successors right into the 19th century. In one

In 1817, members of a European expedition visiting Kumasi marveled at the wealth and magnificence of the Asante royal court. This painting by an expedition artist documents an Asante yam festival.

instance, a man who had begun as a salt carrier rose to the post of minister of foreign affairs. The rulers of Asante kept in touch with their officials through a complex network of messengers, and they also employed Muslim clerks to keep careful records of government affairs—thus they avoided the problems faced by the Yoruba rulers of Oyo, who communicated only by word of mouth.

The kings of Asante also followed the example of other rulers by maintaining a standing army. These troops, known as the Ankobia, were based in Kumasi and were specially designated to maintain order, both within the city and within the empire. Whenever there were signs of revolt among Asante's subject states, the Ankobia could be speedily dispatched to quell the disturbance.

Given the attention to detail displayed by Asante's rulers, it is not surprising that Kumasi—founded, according to Asante tradition, under a sacred tree known as the *kuma*—presented a splendid spectacle to visitors. Even a group of fastidious European traders who traveled to Kumasi in 1817 were impressed by the neatness of the streets and houses and the careful program of sanitation followed by the residents. They also discovered, as 5,000 of Kumasi's 40,000 citizens came out to greet them, that the people of Asante had brought their civilization to a high degree of style and enthusiasm:

> What we had seen on our way [wrote the Englishman William Bowditch] had made us expect something unusual. But we were still surprised by the extent and display of the scene which burst upon us here. An area of nearly a mile in circumference was crowded with magnificence and novelty. The king, his chiefs and captains, were splendidly dressed, and were surrounded by attendants of every kind. More than a hundred bands broke into music on our arrival. At least a hundred large umbrellas, each of which could shelter thirty persons, were sprung up and down by their bearers with a brilliant effect, being made in scarlet, yellow and the brightest cloths and silks, and crowned on top with crescents, pelicans, elephants, barrels, arms and swords of gold.

Such ornaments were just a sample of the Asante's artistic skills. Many of their most striking artifacts were fashioned not from bronze but from gold-plated alloys (combinations of metals), using the forgotten technique of lost-wax casting. As Jean Laude has indicated, the practice of making royal funeral masks and pendant masks most likely originated during the reign of Opoku Ware in the first half of the 18th century and was associated with Akan religious be-

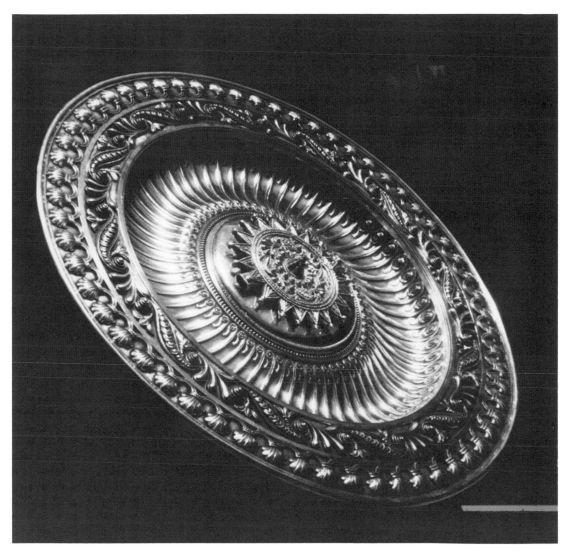

liefs. The Akan maintained that the *okra*, or soul, was divided into two parts: one represented the spirit of the individual and the other a separate being that would watch over him or her through eternity. "Round gold plaques worn on the chest," Laude wrote, "are the soul carriers. Only the bearer of the king's soul (*okrafo*), who had to belong to the sovereign's family, was entitled to wear them. The commemorative masks probably portrayed chiefs or kings killed or

The golden disk in the center of this plate was made to be worn on the chest of an okrafo, *the bearer of an Asante king's soul.*

British soldiers and Asante warriors fight for control of the Gold Coast in 1824. The Asante won this battle, but 50 years later another conflict with the British forced them to relinquish their land.

made prisoners in war. The motif sculpted at the corners of the lips symbolizes the soul (*honhom*) which escapes through the mouth at the moment of death. The Ashanti kings . . . continue to live in Heaven after death. From that vantage point they watch over their people. Golden masks placed on royal tombs prove the permanence of this invisible royalty."

Ultimately, the same Europeans who were so impressed with the achievements of the Asante were to
bring about the downfall of the empire. The visit of
the trading delegation in 1817 convinced the British
government that Asante was a rich source of trade,
and the government took over the coastal forts from
private trading companies in 1821. The Asante

Asante dignitaries carry their staffs of office during a ceremony in modern Ghana, where, despite 57 years of British rule, West African traditions live on.

quickly found cause to resent British policies along the coast: the British made their own arrangements with Asante's subject states, thus weakening the control of the empire.

Nevertheless, the Asante initially tried to tolerate the intruders. As Basil Davidson wrote, "The general approach . . . was to show enough strength to contain European ambitions within what were regarded as reasonable or inevitable limits, and then to make treaties of trade and friendship which, it was hoped, the Europeans would keep. Useful variations on this policy were found in playing off one set of Europeans against another. The kings only fought when all else failed."

The Asante were forced to go to war in 1824, when the British governor, Sir Charles McCarthy, launched a campaign intended to break their grip on the region. The Asante soundly defeated the British, sending McCarthy to his death. For the next half century, the British government steered clear of direct involvement in Asante, while British merchants kept peace with the empire and made vast sums from their holdings along the coast.

Ultimately, the competing empires of Britain and Asante were bound to face each other down. In 1872, the king of Asante sent an expedition to the coast to subdue the defiant vassal states allied with the British. General Tia, the commander of the expedition, at first attempted to negotiate with the British governor, Sir Garnet Wolseley. Tia assured Wolseley that there could be peace between Asante and Britain, if only the British would stop supporting the vassal states (including the always-troublesome Denkyira). Wolseley's response, in 1874, was to begin a full-scale invasion of Asante, which the battle-hardened veteran later called "the most horrible war I ever took part in." With great difficulty, the British forces finally occupied Kumasi and forced the Asante to sign the Treaty of Fomena, which guaranteed the British a free hand along the coast. The Asante rebuilt their ruined capital and attempted to resurrect their empire, but their efforts were finally ended by another British invasion in 1900. The Asante then became subjects of the British Empire and did not regain their independence until the nation of Ghana was formed in 1957.

In all these confrontations with the powers of Europe, the Africans were at a disadvantage because they could not match the technology and political flexibility that Europeans had developed since the end of the Middle Ages in 1500. There are many reasons for this disparity. One is surely the damage done to Africa by the slave trade and the enrichment of the nations that ran it.

On a deeper level, African and European societies were fundamentally different. Simply put, Africans had always remained close to the expansive continent they and their ancestors had tamed, and they believed deeply that their way of life could not be improved on. Africans, Basil Davidson has written, "were the victims of their own success. . . . Towards all questions of fundamental change they showed a fundamental hostility. They were conservative by the strictest definition. . . . Although the outcome of a great deal of daring experiment in the past, they had reached a self-perpetuating level where further large experiment seemed not only unwise, but also, given the spiritual sanctions that helped to stay them up, positively wrong."

Davidson adds that Africa's great political diversity became a fatal handicap in the face of such challenges as the slave trade and colonialism. Africans were completely unprepared to unite against a common enemy; it had never occurred to them that their entire way of life could be threatened by outside forces. They and their ancestors had tamed a vast and beautiful continent that provided them with everything they desired. They had never felt the need, as Europeans had, to build ships and sail out to see what lay beyond the horizon. Confronted by aggressive intruders who had developed the ambition and the tools to remake the world in their own image, the peoples of Africa had little hope of preserving what they had so carefully built up.

With the fall of Asante, the last of the great West African kingdoms faded from view. Africa would have to endure decades of colonial rule before Africans' quest for nationhood became a political reality in the

20th century. Though they lie within different borders, the cities of the ancient kingdoms—Benin, Oyo,
Timbuktu, Jenne, Gao, Kumasi—endure, living relics
of a glorious heritage.

FURTHER READING

Battuta, Ibn. *Travels in Asia and Africa, 1325–1354*. Translated by H. A. R. Gibb. London: Routledge, 1957.

Connah, Graham. *African Civilizations*. Cambridge, England: Cambridge University Press, 1987.

Davidson, Basil. *Africa in History*. Rev. ed. New York: Collier, 1991.

———. *The African Genius*. Boston: Little, Brown, 1969.

———. *Lost Cities of Africa*. Rev. ed. Boston: Little, Brown, 1987.

Davidson, Basil, with F. K. Buah and J. F. A. Ajayi. *A History of West Africa: 1000–1600*. New rev. ed. London: Longman, 1977.

Fage, J. D. *An Atlas of African History*. London: Edward Arnold, 1978.

Hourani, Albert. *A History of the Arab Peoples*. New York: Warner Books, 1991.

Hrbek, I., ed. *Africa from the Seventh to the Eleventh Century*. Vol. 3. UNESCO *General History of Africa*. Abr. ed. Berkeley: University of California Press, 1992.

Hull, Richard W. *African Cities and Towns Before the European Conquest*. New York: Norton, 1976.

Laude, Jean. *The Arts of Black Africa*. Translated by Jean Decock. Berkeley: University of California Press, 1971.

Levtzion, Nehemiah. *Ancient Ghana and Mali*. New York: Africana, 1980.

Levtzion, Nehemiah, and J. F. G. Hopkins. *Corpus of Early Arabic Sources for West African History*. Cambridge, England: Cambridge University Press, 1981.

McLeod, Malcolm D. *The Asante*. London: British Museum Press, 1981.

Oliver, Roland, and Anthony Atmore. *Africa Since 1800*. 3rd ed. Cambridge, England: Cambridge University Press, 1981.

Oliver, Roland, and B. M. Fagan. *Africa in the Iron Age*. Cambridge, England: Cambridge University Press, 1975.

Oliver, Roland, and J. D. Fage. *A Short History of Africa*. 6th ed. New York: Penguin, 1988.

Previté-Orton, C. W. *The Shorter Cambridge Medieval History*. 2 vols. Cambridge, England: Cambridge University Press, 1952.

INDEX

PICTURE CREDITS

PHILIP KOSLOW earned his B.A. and M.A. degrees from New York University and went on to teach and conduct research at Oxford University, where his long-standing interest in medieval European and African history was awakened. The editor of numerous volumes for young readers, he is also the author of *El Cid* in the Chelsea House HISPANICS OF ACHIEVEMENT series and of *The Seminole Indians* in Chelsea House's JUNIOR LIBRARY OF AMERICAN INDIANS. Koslow is currently at work on a comprehensive 10-volume series on the kingdoms of West Africa.

CLAYBORNE CARSON, senior consulting editor of the MILESTONES IN BLACK AMERICAN HISTORY series, is a professor of history at Stanford University. His first book, *In Struggle: SNCC and the Black Awakening of the 1960s* (1981), won the Frederick Jackson Turner Prize of the Organization of American Historians. He is the director of the Martin Luther King, Jr., Papers Project, which will publish 12 volumes of King's writings.

DARLENE CLARK HINE, senior consulting editor of the MILESTONES IN BLACK AMERICAN HISTORY series, is the John A. Hannah Professor of American History at Michigan State University. She is the author of numerous books and articles on black women's history. Her most recent work is the two-volume *Black Women in America: An Historical Encyclopedia* (1993).

THE CONCEPT OF STRUCTURALISM

To my mother and father

Philip Pettit

THE CONCEPT OF STRUCTURALISM:
A Critical Analysis

UNIVERSITY OF CALIFORNIA PRESS
Berkeley and Los Angeles 1975

UNIVERSITY OF CALIFORNIA PRESS
Berkeley and Los Angeles, California

ISBN: 0 – 520 – 02882 – 1
Library of Congress Catalog Card Number: 74–22971

© Philip Pettit 1975

Printed and bound in Great Britain

Contents

Preface

'STRUCTURALISM' claims to provide a framework for organising and orientating any 'semiological' study, any study concerned with the production and perception of 'meaning'. It derives the framework from linguistics, the primary semiological discipline, and extends it to the analysis of the literary arts, the analysis of the non-literary arts and the analysis, in social psychology and social anthropology, of 'customary arts'.

The framework deserves the attention of the practitioners and philosophers of linguistics and these other disciplines. I argue that, with the possible exception of linguistics, the framework will not make a 'science' of any of these disciplines. What it can do however is give them the means of being organised in their analysis, going beyond *ad hoc* observations.

My essay is in four chapters. The first examines the framework available to structuralists from linguistics : I call the framework, the 'linguistic model'. The second chapter considers the possible range of this model in other semiological disciplines. The third criticises the development of the model proposed by Lévi-Strauss; and the fourth offers an evaluation of the part which such a model can play in the advance of knowledge. I have divided the chapters into sections and each of these is described in the analysis of contents (pp. viii-x).

This is a theoretical essay, not a historical one, as my interest is in the concept of structuralism rather than the structuralist movement. I have not found it possible, however, to avoid history entirely. In the first chapter I discuss Saussure, Jakobson and Chomsky since their theories are, inevitably, the source of the linguistic model. In the second chapter I discuss various thinkers whose work, wittingly or not, illustrates the extension of the linguistic model to non-linguistic fields. Among these thinkers are self-styled structuralists like Barthes and Todorov but also thinkers who would not normally rank as structuralists: this is a varied group and includes people as diverse as Rudolf Arnheim, Christian Norberg-Schulz, Harold Garfinkel and Erving Goffman. In the third chapter I discuss Lévi-Strauss since his work is often taken as a paradigm of a structuralist approach and I also comment on the work of Althusser, Foucault and Lacan.

Being essentially theoretical, the essay does not claim to be a piece of sharp scholarship. I have quoted from translations where these were available—the sources are usually French—and made amendments only in a few places; where no translation was available I have made my own. Saussurian scholarship is particularly tortuous and I have been careful to avoid the controversial issues. I provide a bibliography for each chapter in the list of references at the end. Where a book referred to in one chapter is listed at the end of another I indicate this in the referring note by adding 'cited above (or below) in X', 'X' being the chapter at the end of which the book is listed.

The essay took the form of a lecture course at Cambridge in the Lent term 1974 and I am grateful to the audience for forcing me to some degree of clarity. I am grateful also to the many friends who were good enough to comment on drafts of the text or discuss ideas contained in it. This must be a nearly complete list: Eileen Barker, Kevin Barry, Joe Cremona, Jonathan Culler, Stephen Heath, Mary Hesse, Peter Holland, Caroline Humphrey, Mary Kelly, Joel Kupperman, Colin McCabe, Graham MacDonald, Christine MacLeod, Ernan McMullin, John Maguire, Paddy Masterson, David Reason, Eva Schaper and Denys Turner. Jonathan Culler was particularly helpful as a guide to structuralist sources and Christine MacLeod as a guide to style. Finally, I must express my gratitude to Mr Pauley and Mrs Smith: while I wrote this, they sustained me in a College existence.

Trinity Hall, Cambridge
March 1974

Analysis of Contents

I THE LINGUISTIC MODEL

1. The linguistic sources of structuralism. Strategy for analysis.
2. The conceptual theory of language in question, not the empirical.
3. Saussure's definition of the object of linguistic investigation : language, not speaking; language taken synchronically, not diachronically.
4. Saussure's account of the linguistic sign. The critique of nominalism. Signifier and signified. Form and matter.
5. The differentiation of the sign. Language as a 'system of differences'.
6. Saussure's distinction between the paradigmatic and syntagmatic relationships of every sign.
7. A scientific linguistics? Two possible strategies, paradigmatic and syntagmatic.
8. The paradigmatic strategy in Jakobson's structural phonology and in structural semantics.
9. Saussure's view of syntax an obstacle to the syntagmatic strategy.
10. Chomsky's generative syntax as part of a syntagmatic strategy.
11. A Saussurian model of language. The debt to Chomsky.
12. Looking for a differential semantics, the other part of a syntagmatic strategy : this, the task of sections 13, 14, 15, 16.
13. The categorial structure of sentences.
14. The subcategorial structure of sentences.
15. The story suggested about sentence construction and sentence interpretation. Articulation and attention.
16. Differential semantics—and the established competitors. Three models for structuralist analysis outside linguistics : structural phonology, generative syntax and differential semantics.

II THE RANGE OF THE MODEL

17. Structuralism and semiology.
18. Meaning and mechanism in language.
19. Meaning and mechanism in other semiological areas. Preliminary examples.
20. The humanist objection to structuralism. The debate with phenomenology.
21. The Homeomorphic use of the linguistic model in stylistics.
22. The possibilities of its paramorphic use : in the literary, the non-literary and the customary arts. The options in a semiology of the literary narrative :
23. 'Straight' analysis.
24. Generative theory.
25. Descriptive theory.
26. Systematic analysis.
27. The tree of options in summary. Figure 1.
28. The semiology of non-literary art. The options :
29. 'Straight' analysis. The commutation test.
30. The case against theory.
31. Systematic analysis. The problem of categories.
32. The semiology of customary art. The arts of cuisine, fashion and presentation.
33. The options in this semiology.

III A DEVELOPMENT OF THE MODEL

34. The 'anti-phenomenologists' : Althusser, Foucault, Lacan— and Lévi-Strauss.
35. Lévi-Strauss's analysis of kinship and myth. Only the latter semiological.
36. Two obstacles to the orthodox analysis of myth.
37. Lévi-Strauss's project : the obstacles by-passed.
38. The phonological model behind this project. Universalism and binarism.
39. Lévi-Strauss's philosophy. The reductionism in this.
40. The determinism.
41. The musical illustration.
42. Lévi-Strauss's theory of myth.
43. Lévi-Strauss's method of myth analysis. Oedipus analysis.
44. The method as a way of by-passing the obstacles mentioned in section 36.

I

The Linguistic Model

1. Structuralism takes its starting point from language. It derives from linguistics a framework of concepts which it seeks to extend from language to the other areas of its interest: to the literary arts, the non-literary arts and the 'customary arts'. This framework of concepts I call the 'linguistic model'.

The linguistics which provides structualism with its model is, in the broadest sense, structural linguistics. In this sense structural linguistics includes most twentieth-century theoretical linguistics. It contrasts with the older tradition of examining languages comparatively, with little theoretical guidance on what to investigate. The master of structural linguistics, at least on the structuralist reading, is Ferdinand de Saussure, the Swiss linguist of the early part of the century. Structuralists have drawn heavily on his theoretical ideas. They have also drawn on the more specialised ideas of recent linguists: Roman Jakobson for example in phonology, Noam Chomsky in grammar (see Lepschy).

In this chapter I want to describe a model of language which structuralists are in a position to derive from structural linguistics. There are two conditions which I put on the model. The first, naturally enough, is that it should be plausible. The second is that it should be grounded in the work of Saussure and other structural linguists, especially Jakobson and Chomsky whom I consider to be the most important figures since Saussure.[1] I am not sure that the model I describe is the only one which satisfies those conditions but, for our purpose, it is as good as any I can envisage.

1. This judgment explains in part why I do not discuss Hjelmslev and Martinet. The other part of the explanation is that everything in semiology which can be described in their terms can be equally well described in Jakobson's.

That purpose is to be able to understand the project of extending structural linguistic concepts to other areas. In the next chapter we shall examine this project, looking at various uses that may be made in non-linguistic areas of the model of language described here. If the first condition is fulfilled, and the model is a plausible one, that examination will have an intrinsic theoretical interest. If the second condition is fulfilled, and the model does significantly reflect the tradition of structural linguistics, the examination will have the added historical interest that we may be able to illustrate the different uses of the model in the actual enterprises of structuralists inspired by that tradition.

About Jakobson and Chomsky, whose work is extremely complex, I should say that I do not intend to discuss in detail the substance of their theories, or the relation between those theories. In Jakobson's structural phonology I find a linguistic strategy that represents one use of the model of language to be found in Saussure. In Chomsky's generative syntax I find a strategy which, at another level, also represents a use of that model—though now a model significantly amended. I am only interested in their theories to the extent that they show how the model may be used in research, and with what amendments. I ignore questions such as how precisely each theory is to be developed, how they fit together, whether there is a generative phonology, and so on.

2. There is a point of method which I must clarify right away. This is that I regard the argument for the 'Saussurian' linguistic model—and the argument for its extension to other areas—as a conceptual or philosophical type of argument. I have no interest in keeping philosophy apart from empirical disciplines, in keeping conceptual analysis apart from the analysis of facts. On the contrary, I believe that the two belong together, that philosophy without empirical disciplines is empty, empirical disciplines without philosophy are blind. It remains true however that there is something distinctive about philosophy; conceptual analysis just is not the analysis of facts.

Philosophy, I will say, is concerned with setting up a conceptual framework within which a range of facts can be characterised; this at least is one philosophical concern. Take the facts of usage about any particular language. A linguist will characterise these by drawing on concepts like phoneme, word, sentence, phonological structure, grammatical structure, and so on. Unless he can characterise them in such systematically ordered concepts, he will not be able to set them up for empirical analysis. What I want to suggest is that the framework of concepts underliying the linguist's empirical or scientific analysis is the product of philosophical argument.

What is this argument? Certainly it is not the appeal, typical of science, to what the facts are like. If I am arguing that a particular set of concepts is the best one for representing linguistic facts, I do of course appeal to the facts to show that they lend themselves to such representaion : I argue for example that none of the distinctions introduced by the concepts is impossible to maintain. This appeal to the facts however does not show why they should be represented in the recommended way, why the new distinctions should be introduced. To argue for that conclusion I must make a distinctively philosophical appeal to how it is necessary to conceive of the facts if it is going to seem possible that something or other should be the case. I might argue in the linguistic example: 'granted that speakers can do this or that, here is how we must conceive of the facts about language; the alternative ways of looking at the facts make it difficult to see how the speakers can have the ability in question'.

In this chapter I am concerned with what I take to be a philosophical level of argument. The 'Saussurian' model is a conceptual framework to be defended on the sort of grounds indicated. Take one feature of the framework which no structural linguist would contest : the assumption that where there is meaning—in a word or a sentence—there is structure, the word being restricted by the rules to a particular set of uses, the sentence to a particular set of interpretations. The argument behind this assumption is that if language were not structured, if the use of language were not bound by rules, it is difficult to see how speakers could give a common meaning to words and sentences. The argument may seem obvious but it has not always been accepted. Think of the 'nominalists' whom Wittgenstein may have expected to surprise. 'I say the sentence : "The weather is fine"; but the words are after all arbitrary signs—so let's put "a b c d" in their place. But now when I read this, I can't connect it straight away with the above sense' (Wittgenstein 139).

The argument that meaning requires structure is basic to the model of language traditional in structural linguistics but it leaves the model vague : we know that language is structured in such a way that differences of meaning in words or sentences reflect structural differences, but we know nothing specific about the structure. I am concerned in this chapter with two philosophical arguments which bear on the type of structure involved in language. The first is in Saussure and suggests that the structure is essentially 'differential', the second is in Chomsky and says that it is essentially 'generative'. What I want to show is that the arguments are not necessarily in conflict and that out of them we can get a model of language of the sort presupposed by structuralism.

3.   To begin with Saussure : he takes linguistics in its most proper sense to be concerned with 'language' rather than 'speaking', and with language seen 'synchronically' rather than 'diachronically'. Both of these specifications need some spelling out.

The distinction between language and speaking is better known in the French terms as the distinction between *langue* and *parole*. To draw the distinction quickly, speaking is something we do individually, language is something we have in common that enables us to speak. Speaking therefore represents one's personal freedom, language a social institution (Saussure—henceforth S—18–19, 76–7, 124–5). Many problems have been raised with this distinction, mainly problems to do with what exactly belongs to language and what to speaking (see Spence). The distinction coincides roughly with that between code and message and it has affinities with Chomsky's distinction between linguistic competence and linguistic performance : language is the code in which the messages of speech are cast, it exists as a form of competence which I exercise—perhaps imperfectly—in the performance of speech. The distinction serves an important purpose in Saussure because it enables him to define an appropriate object for linguistic investigation. Language is that object and it is appropriate because, unlike speaking, it is relatively stable and does not shift with the personal style of each speaker (S 19–20).

A qualification is necessary however : language changes over time, under different pressures, and is not strictly a stable object of analysis. This observation presses Saussure to specify more narrowly the object of linguistics proper, as language considered synchronically or statically; this he distinguishes from language considered diachronically, as it has developed through time (S 79–100). As in the case of the previous distinction the principle is clear but its application raises difficulties. Questions may be raised about what is to count as a single language, what as a state of that language, what as a time over which no significant development takes place, and so on (see Ducrot/Todorov 179–81). All we need to remark is that linguistics proper is synchronic and that this is presupposed by any interesting diachronic study : the significance of a change can be understood only if the termini are understood. The primary object of linguistic investigation is a language rather than the speaking of it, and a language considered in its state at a particular time.[2]

4. We turn now to language understood in this restricted sense. Saussure takes it that the basic elements of language are linguistic signs; in effect, words—that is, words in the sense in which variants like 'do' and 'does' are different words.[3] His first priority is to undermine the nominalist view that words have meaning through standing as names for things : 'people see nothing more than a name-giving system in language, thereby prohibiting any research into its true nature' (S 16). His objection to the view is put in three points. 'It assumes that ready-made ideas exist before words; it does not tell us whether a name is vocal or psychological in nature . . .; finally, it lets us assume that the linking of a name and a thing is a very simple operation—an assumption that is anything but true' (S 65). The first point in the objection—that there are no ideas before words—is the crucial one for Saussure : 'psychologically our thought—apart

2. Saussure does admit diachronic linguistics of course and even a linguistics of speaking; an example of this latter, he thinks, is speech physiology (S 32–7).
3. In fact Saussure often uses 'words' in the other sense (S 105; but see Godel 269). For that reason he finds them too 'abstract' to count as linguistic signs, 'the concrete entities of our science' (S 102). He also finds them too 'complex', since they include examples like 'painful' and 'delightful' (S 106). Nevertheless he is prepared, for convenience, to speak of 'words' in preference to 'linguistic signs' (S 110–11).

from its expression in words—is only a shapeless and indistinct mass' (S 111).

If it is not necessarily the name of a thing, then what are the essential features of a word, what are the features which will explain how it comes to have meaning? Saussure makes two distinctions in response to this question. The first is between signified (*signifié*) and signifier (*signifiant*), the second between form and matter. The distinctions cross one another so that in each word we have four factors to take into consideration : the form and matter of the signifier and the form and matter of the signified. We shall see in the next section that the most important factor in a word is its form, in particular the form of its signified. It is this which defines the meaning of the word and we shall be asking what determines it.

First, the distinction between signified and signifier. Saussure thinks that every word unites a phonic element and an element of thought, a sound and a concept. 'The linguistic sign unites, not a thing and a name, but a concept and a sound image' (S 66). The sound in which the word consists is the signifier, the concept is the signified (S 67). Saussure insists that these two elements cannot be taken apart without destroying the word. Take any word and you will find that it represents not only a distinct concept but a distinct sound : similarly for the written word. This is not just a matter of fact, but a matter of necessity. 'In language, a concept is a quality of its phonic substance just as a particular slice of sound is a quality of the concept' (S 103). Saussure means that if in a language at any period you change the signifier element in a word you will also change the element signified; if you change the element signified—and you still claim to speak the public language—you will have to change the signifier element. He illustrates the point in a famous image. 'Language can also be compared with a sheet of paper : thought is the front and the sound is the back; one cannot cut the front without cutting the back at the same time' (S 113).

The second distinction on which Saussure draws in marking off the different factors in a word is a fairly traditional one, that between form and matter. He likes to present it by means of examples. Consider the train which we know as 'the 8.25 p.m. from Geneva to Paris'. We say that this is the same train from day to day, even though the carriages and engine may change regularly. What remains the same is the form of the train; it is only the matter that changes (S 108). Again, consider a chess knight. 'Suppose that the piece happens to be destroyed or lost during a game. Can it be replaced by an equivalent piece? Certainly. Not only another knight but even a figure shorn of any resemblance to a knight can be declared identical provided the same value is attributed to it' (S 110). What remains the same is the form of the chess piece; again the matter changes. Saussure finds a similar situation with words. Take the word 'gentlemen'. This may vary in the way it is pronounced, and it may vary in the way it is meant; yet it remains one and the same word. What varies is the phonic and psychological matter; the form of the word—as sound and concept—remains the same (S 109).

5.   There are four factors involved in each word then : the form and matter of the signifier and the form and matter of the signified. The factors in which Saussure is interested as a linguist are the formal ones. His main linguistic question is, what gives a word its distinctive phonic and conceptual form? He assumes that to answer this question will be to answer the question, how does a word come to have its particular meaning?

Saussure's answer to the question about form is that the systematic differentiation of any particular word from other words gives it its distinctive form. 'Sister' is differentiated in sound from 'mister' and 'cistern' for example; it is differentiated conceptually from 'mother', 'daughter', 'wife' and so on. The differences which hold a word off from other words—most conspicuously the differences which hold it off from closely related words—give the word its own identity. Thus the English word 'sheep' does not quite coincide with its French translation *mouton* because the English word stands off from the differentiated word 'mutton' and there is no word which corresponds to this in French (S 115–16).

The differentiation which gives each word its form or identity is systematic for Saussure because it is controlled by language. Language is precisely a set of words which are systematically differentiated from one another, in sound and conceptually. But even this formulation can be misleading : it suggests that the words exist prior to their differentiation. A stone is already a stone before it becomes marked off as the cornerstone of a particular building. Before a word is marked off in language it is nothing distinct, just nebulous thought and sound. In view of this Saussure says that language is a set of differences rather than a set of differentiated terms. 'A difference generally implies positive terms between which the difference is set up; but in language there are only differences without positive terms . . . A linguistic system is a series of differences of sound combined with a series of differences of ideas' (S 120).

Here we have Saussure's basic conceptual point : language necessarily involves differential structure. The point is that it is difficult to see how words could remain identifiably the same, over shifts in pronunciation and use, if they did not have a formal identity established within language—specifically, by their differentiation from other words. Language, he concludes, is first and foremost a system for differentiating words.

6.   Saussure is more specific than this about the differentiation of words in language. He says that the differentiation takes place within two kinds of relationship that any word is given by its language, referring to these as 'associative'—I shall say 'paradigmatic'—and 'syntagmatic' relationships (S 123–34). Such relationships exist between words considered as sounds and between words considered as concepts. I shall discuss them only as they exist between words considered as concepts.

The syntagmatic relationships of a word are those it has with words which can occur in its neighbourhood in a sentence. There is a syntagmatic relationship between 'John' and 'dances' which allows the words to appear in the sentence 'John dances . . .'. The relationship in question is like that between any two words, the first of which can appear as subject to the second : for example, between 'he' and 'plays', 'river' and 'flows', 'dog' and 'bites'. Such a relationship does not exist between two nouns or two verbs since we do not get 'Dog river . . .' or 'Plays flows . . .'. Also it does not exist between every noun (or pronoun) and every verb : we do not normally find '(The) river bites . . .' or '(The) dog flows . . .'.

Its syntagmatic relationships are clearly essential to a word. If a word lost some such relationships or gained others it would lose its old formal identity, it would become a different word :

thus 'flows' would not be the word it is if it could take 'plays' in its subject place or if, in ordinary usage, it could take 'dog' in its subject place.[4] For Saussure the way to put this is to say that the differences between a word and those other words with which it occurs in recognised 'syntagms' are crucial to the definition of the word. 'In the syntagm a term acquires its value only because it stands in opposition to everything that precedes or follows it, or to both' (S 123).

The paradigmatic relationships of a word are less clearly defined by Saussure than the syntagmatic. They include all the essential relationships which a word has outside its syntagmatic ones and they isolate another range of differences which are crucial in the definition of the word. Take the word 'flows' again. It has essential syntagmatic relationships with its possible subjects —for example 'river', 'time', 'thought'—and its possible adverbs : 'quickly', 'smoothly', 'silently'. Correspondingly however it has relationships with words which may have the same subjects and the same adverbs : for example with 'flees', 'moves' and 'runs'. It has weaker relationships of the same kind with words which may have the same subjects but not the same adverbs, or the same adverbs but not the same subjects. All of these relationships are non-syntagmatic because the words between which they hold cannot occur in the neighbourhood of one another—at least when 'neighbourhood' is strictly understood. The relationships are essential however in the sense that if a word lost some such relationships or gained others it would lose its old formal identity : if there were no word 'flee' the word 'flow' would become a subtly different word. These relationships of a word are its paradigmatic ones.

It is usual to think of the paradigmatic relationships of a word as those it has with words which may replace it in some sentence without making the sentence syntagmatically unacceptable; these relationships are non-syntagmatic since words which may replace one another do not occur in the neighbourhood of one another. Saussure suggests this way of thinking of paradigmatic relationships in his discussion of sentence construction and sentence interpretation (see section 9 below). Elsewhere he does present

---

4. Whether or not Saussure allows it, such a shift of meaning is possible through the literal acceptance of metaphorical usage (see section 52 below).

them as any relationships of psychological association between words which are unrelated syntagmatically: thus *enseignement* is associatively related with its variants *enseigner* and *enseignons*, and with its synonyms *apprentissage* and *education* (S 123). We shall take paradigmatic relationships in the first of these two senses (see Lyons 1969, 74–6).

Like syntagmatic relationships, paradigmatic ones isolate differences which are crucial in the definition of any word within the language. Just as a word must be linguistically differentiated from those words with which it occurs in a 'syntagm' so it must be differentiated from those words which may replace it in some syntagmatic context without making nonsense. Thus 'flees' may replace 'flows' in many of the contexts in which it occurs and it is vital for the exact definition of either word that they be differentiated from one another within the language. Unless there is some established respect in which they contrast, the words will merge into one another and lose their individual identities.

7. Saussure's model of language now presents itself in some perspective. Language—that is, language as distinct from speaking, language synchronically considered—is essentially a system for differentiating words. It differentiates them by setting up syntagmatic and paradigmatic relationships within which any word is marked off from other words and receives an identity of its own.

This model suggests a programme for linguistics because it takes the mystery out of language, it puts language among the things of the material world. Like many other realities language is a system; Saussure also says, a mechanism or organism. 'Language is a system of interdependent terms in which the value of each term results solely from the simultaneous presence of the others' (S 114). This system is not even distinguished by being a product of the conscious mind; it works by unconscious laws. 'The system is a complex mechanism that can be grasped only through reflection; the very ones who use it daily are ignorant of it' (S 73).

Saussure makes only the outline of his envisaged linguistics clear. It stands off from the study of speaking or of linguistic development. It takes up within itself traditional disciplines like morphology, syntax, and lexicology (S 134–6). Its concern is everywhere the same: to reveal in language the systematic relating of terms on the paradigmatic and syntagmatic axes. 'The aim of general synchronic linguistics is to set up the fundamental principles of any idiosynchronic system, the constituents of any language-state' (S 101).

If we think of going beyond Saussure and filling in this outline, it becomes apparent that there are two quite different approaches which his model might suggest for linguistics: I shall call them, the paradigmatic and syntagmatic approaches. The distinction between the two is important and will recur throughout this essay. Here I want to give a brief formal characterisation of each approach; this will be complemented by concrete illustration in the coming sections.

The paradigmatic approach would follow this strategy:

1. find distinctive features by reference to which any linguistic term may be differentiated from any other; the terms will differ in respect of which of these features they have and which they have not,

2. assign a characterisation in terms of these features to each term so that the term is sufficiently differentiated from every other term,

3. formulate syntagmatic laws governing which terms—that is, the terms with which features—may combine with which,

4. isolate the differences between terms, which are important paradigmatically: the differences between terms which may replace one another.

I call this approach the paradigmatic one because the features by means of which the linguistic terms are described are the features which define the paradigmatic differences between terms.

The syntagmatic approach does not attempt to describe each linguistic term in such specific features. Its strategy is to describe the terms in abstract features—for instance as 'noun phrase', 'verb phrase' and so on—for the purposes of formulating syntagmatic laws and to resort to more specific terms for the purposes of describing the paradigmatically important differences between terms. The steps of the strategy are:

1. find abstract features by reference to which any linguistic term may be characterised, being identified with some terms, differentiated from others,

2. assign a characterisation in terms of these features to each term so that it is clear what sort of term it is,

3. formulate syntagmatic laws governing which sorts of terms may combine with which,

4. isolate—for a given combination of terms—the differences which are important in marking off each term paradigmatically from those which may replace it.

8.   The paradigmatic approach is the one nearest to the spirit of Saussure. It is the approach which was adopted by Jakobson and the Prague school of phonology in the late 1920s and early 1930s (see Jakobson, Trubetzkoy; also Ivic). Jakobson and the other Prague phonologists broke with Saussure in considering language just as a phonic system, putting aside its conceptual aspect. They took from him however the idea that, essentially, the structure of language is differential; and, more particularly, the idea that differentiation takes place on two axes, the paradigmatic and the syntagmatic.

Within a phonological programme the word could not be seen as the basic linguistic unit. Its place was taken by the phoneme. This may be defined as the minimal discrete unit of sound which cannot vary without changing the word to which it belongs. The phoneme is taken to remain the same over standard differences in pronunciation and standard variations in stress, so phonemic variation is by definition significant (see Kramsky).

The Prague strategy was exactly the paradigmatic one. They found the distinctive features they required in voice, nasality, labiality, dentality, velarity and so on. They could assign a characterisation to each phoneme by putting the features in a list and marking the phoneme plus ($+$) or minus ($-$) for each feature—or, where the feature was irrelevant, nought (o); thus the phoneme could be characterised by an ordered set of pluses, minuses and noughts. With such characterisations available the phonologists could begin to formulate the syntagmatic laws governing phonemic combination : roughly, laws of the form— phonemes with certain features do not occur in a certain position in the neighbourhood of phonemes with certain other features. Finally, the phonologists could go on to isolate the differences between phonemes—the differences constituted by a variation in certain features—which were important paradigmatically.

One other linguistic 'school' took a paradigmatic approach to language, though not so systematically or so successfully as the school of structural phonology. I am thinking of the mixed group of linguists who describe their work as 'structural semantics' or, less often, 'componential analysis' (see Berlin/Kay, Goodenough, Lyons 1963, Scheffler/Lounsbury, Trier). Structural semantics disavows the Saussurian goal of a unified linguistic theory, also the Jakobsonian goal of a partial but still systematic theory. Its interest is in areas of vocabulary, 'lexical fields', which are selected more or less at random : thus Berlin and Kay deal with the lexical field of colour terms. The idea is to find features by means of which the terms may be differentiated from one another, each term being characterised according to the features it does and does not have. Steps 1 and 2 in the paradigmatic strategy are followed exactly but not 3 and 4 : the area chosen for analysis in any particular case is too restricted to make the search for syntagmatic laws or crucial paradigmatic differences meaningful.

The best formulation of the principle directing structural semantics is still Trier's. 'The value of a word is first recognised when one sets it against the value of neighbouring and opposed words. The word has meaning only as part of the whole' (Trier 6). The idea is clearly in line with everything Saussure says about the differentiation of linguistic terms. Saussure speaks like some of the structural semanticists in comments which he makes on various examples : for instance when he says that *redouter, craindre, avoir peur*—'to dread', 'to fear' and 'to be afraid'— are crucial to one another; if one disappeared the others would shift in value to compensate for its loss (S 116).

9.   The alternative approach to the paradigmatic is the syntagmatic one. I shall argue in the next section that this is the approach adopted in Chomsky's grammar. In this section I would like to show why it is farther from the spirit of Saussure than the paradigmatic one.

The syntagmatic strategy essentially involves the idea of syntax. It supposes that it is possible to formulate rules which will say, by reference to the characterisation of the elements—as noun phrase, verb phrase, and so on—whether a given syntagmatic combination is allowable or not. The body of such rules would constitute a syntax in the traditional 'rationalist' sense of the term. Saussure rejects the idea of such a syntax because it seems to him to be too abstract, too spiritual; in his eyes it would bring the mystery back into language and put in question the picture of language as a mechanism. 'To think that there is an incorporeal syntax outside material units distributed in space would be a mistake' (S 139).

Saussure feels bound to put something in place of syntax because he toys with the idea of a syntagmatic strategy. On that strategy a word is defined within any combination of words by its contrasts with potential replacements. If syntax is allowed then it can be said that my knowledge of it reveals what may replace any word. Saussure cannot appeal to that knowledge. He appeals instead to my memory that the combinations given by the potential replacements are indeed legitimate combinations.

Saussure says that anyone who knows a language stores in his memory 'specimens' of legitimate combinations of words. When he is presented with a given combination, therefore, he knows whether some word may replace a word in the combination, by reference to his memory of whether the combination which the new word would yield is legitimate. This memory theory suggests a story about sentence construction—as it suggests a story about sentence interpretation—which Saussure illustrates in a discussion of one-word sentences; in the discussion he treats word parts as he might treat words in other examples. 'Our memory holds in reserve all the more or less complex types of syntagms, regardless of their class or length, and we bring in the associative groups to fix our choice when the time for using them arrives. When a Frenchman says '*Marchons!*' '(Let's) walk!' he thinks unconsciously of diverse groups of associations that converge on the syntagm '*Marchons!*'. The syntagm figures in the series '*Marche!*' '(Thou) walk!', '*Marchez!*' '(You) walk!' and the opposition between '*Marchons!*' and the other forms determines his choice; in addition, '*Marchons!*' calls up the series '*Montons!*' '(Let's) go up!', '*Mangeons!*' '(Let's) eat!', etc., and is selected from the series by the same process. In each series the speaker knows what he must vary in order to produce the differentiation that fits the desired unit. If he changes the idea to be expressed, he will need other oppositions to bring out another value; for instance, he may say '*Marchez!*' or perhaps '*Montons!*' (S 130).

Saussure's memory theory seems plausible because the syntagmatic combinations he mentions are so simple and short. The problem is that he must also consider complex sentences. Every sentence, no matter what its complexity, sets up syntagmatic constraints on what word may replace any other and Saussure has to explain how we grasp those constraints. His memory theory will not do this because a sentence may be quite novel in its pattern of word combination, and in that case we cannot rely on memory to tell us whether the sentences which would result from certain word replacements are allowed or not. (In fact Saussure does not think that his theory needs to be applied to anything other than non-complex phrases and sentences. He ignores the fact that every sentence is subject to rules of language and says that it may represent the free—that is, linguistically unconstrained—combining of words by the speaker (S 124).)

10. Of the two approaches consistent with the Saussurian model of language we may assume that only the syntagmatic one holds out the promise of a systematic theory of language proper; the paradigmatic approach does not look like giving a systematic theory outside phonology, where language is considered just as a system of sounds, not of words. The syntagmatic approach is not in the spirit of Saussure however because it involves the idea of syntax. The syntagmatic approach, I now want to say, is carried through in Chomsky's work where a new conception of syntax is elaborated.[5]

First it may be useful to mention one of the things that makes Chomsky's conception new. It is that he thinks of syntax as a body of recursive rules. The idea of the recursive rule was not available to linguists until after the 1930s when logicians had

5. It is a convenient fiction to take Chomsky's starting point as Saussure. It was in fact Bloomfield and other American 'structuralist' linguists. Their approach might be taken as a paradigmatic one, a grammatical reflection of Jakobson's approach in phonology: 'Its fundamental assumption is that procedures of segmentation and classification, applied to data in a systematic way, can isolate and identify all types of elements that function in a particular language along with the constraints that they obey. A catalogue of these elements, their relations, and their restrictions of "distribution", would, in most structuralist views, constitute a full grammar of the language' (Chomsky 1966, 6). Chomsky rejects this approach—as he rejects Saussure (Chomsky 1970, 214).

explored it properly (Chomsky 1965, 8). It is a rule which can apply over and over in a single operation so that, though quite simple itself, it may yield powerful results. Take a rule that a logician might give for interpreting 'not not p' : the rule that it is equivalent to 'p'. Consider now a formula of some complexity, 'not not not not not p'. The rule applies to this recursively to give first 'not not not not p', then 'not not p' and finally 'p' as the interpretation of the formula. A recursive rule in syntax—say a rule that a noun phrase and a verb phrase in a certain order make a sentence—might be invoked a number of times in the process of giving a syntactical description of a sentence : it might apply to any number of embedded or nested sentences before applying to the original sentence itself. The recursive rule can do double or multiple duty and so a syntax built on recursive rules looks a much more plausible prospect than a syntax with something approaching a rule for every case. It might even have looked a plausible prospect to Saussure.

What Chomsky offers is a 'generative syntax', the core of a 'generative grammar'; he thinks of the 'grammar' as including also a (non-generative) phonology and 'semantics' but I shall equate it with 'syntax' (Chomsky 1965, 141). A generative grammar or syntax is a body of recursive rules by means of which any sentence of the language—and only a sentence of the language—can be given an abstract 'structural' description. This description shows what sort of combination the sentence represents, indicating what sorts of words may replace any given word in the sentence. When the grammar can provide such a description for a sentence it is said to 'generate' the sentence or the structure described in the sentence. Hence Chomsky's definition of a generative grammar : 'a system of rules that can iterate to generate an indefinitely large number of structures' (Chomsky 1965, 15–16).

To look for a generative grammar in this sense is to adopt the syntagmatic approach to language. Consider the syntagmatic strategy described in section 7. To write a generative grammar is to have gone through steps 1 and 2 : to have found a set of abstract or structural features for characterising linguistic terms and to have assigned, in principle, a characterisation to every term—that of noun, verb or adverb perhaps or, more concretely, abstract noun, transitive verb, or adverb of motion. It is to be at step 3 in the syntagmatic strategy, to be formulating syntagmatic laws governing which sorts of terms may combine with which. Any combination of terms is allowable which yields, on its own or with other terms, a sentence to which a grammar for the language assigns a structural description.[6]

11. We must take stock of our position. In the last section we argued that the Saussurian model of language can be extended to encompass Chomsky's generative grammar. That grammar comes out as an implementation of the syntagmatic approach described in section 7. The model has to be extended to accommodate this grammar in the sense that it has to become open to the idea of syntax criticised by Saussure.

The Saussurian model was introduced in section 5 on a philosophical argument : that it is difficult to see how words could remain identifiably the same if language did not formally identify them, within a system of differentiation. It is worth remarking that the model has been extended to encompass Chomsky by a similar sort of argument. The argument was suggested in section 9 : that it is difficult to see how people could understand novel sentences if language did not have a generative structure. Language is said to have a generative structure in the sense that knowledge of the language includes knowledge of rules of the kind represented (under idealisation) in the rules of a generative grammar for the language (Chomsky 1965, 4, 15).[7] The argument is that if we do not postulate such knowledge in the speakers/hearers of a language, we have no way of explaining how they know what sort of combination of words is represented in a novel sentence; Saussure's appeal to memory cannot possibly explain this. The argument about generative structure plays the role in Chomsky that the argument about differential structure plays in Saussure.

But we must be clear about what we are and are not taking from Chomsky. We are taking the single argument mentioned

6. Though grammatically allowable the combination might not be acceptable for other reasons such as length, but this does not concern us (see Chomsky 1965, 11).

7. There may be more than one generative grammar for a language, more than one grammar which can assign a structural description to all and only the sentences of the language. Chomsky wants to decide between such grammars on the basis of which fits in best with his account of the 'universal grammar' mentioned later in section 11 (Chomsky 1969, 34–47).

and, as we shall see in sections 13 and 14, Chomsky's broad assessment of its implications. What we are not taking—and two things deserve mention—is, first, another philosophical argument which Chomsky uses in developing his theory. This is the argument that one component of linguistic competence must be innate, that apart from the particular grammar which the native speaker picks up within his culture there must be a universal grammar of which he is the natural master. Unless there were some innate competence, Chomsky says, unless there were a universal grammar, it is hard to see how the child could learn language on the basis of what he hears (see Chomsky 1959). We are not taking this argument from Chomsky because it is not of direct concern to us.

Secondly, and more significantly, we are not taking from him any empirically open views of how language is best represented. Should syntax be represented as split into two parts, one to describe the deep structure of a sentence, the other to show how this transforms into a surface structure (see Winograd 21, 42–3)? Should the structural description given by syntax be represented as presupposing some 'semantic' consideration of the sentence, some consideration of what it means (see McCawley)?[8] I do not wish to prejudge such questions, which have been put to Chomsky by recent critics. The point we are taking from Chomsky is a point which even those critics would concede.

12.   Our conclusion so far is that language is at once differential and generative, that Saussure does not rule out Chomsky. This conclusion gives a picture of language as a system which enables the speaker/hearer first to see the syntagmatic constraints of a

---

8.   Here I give only a rough indication of what distinguishes Chomsky and McCawley, or the autonomous theory and the semantic theory of syntax (for a good account of the difference see Seuren, especially his own essay in chapter 4). The semantic theory claims, as I indicate, that syntax should consider data of meaning as well as data of well-formedness. This is because what syntax is said to do, essentially, is provide semantic representations of the sentences of a language: that is, representations under which the way to their interpretation (in semantics itself, as I use that term in section 16) is open. It is not clear that Chomsky has to reject this account, stated abstractly, of the sources of evidence, and semantic task, of syntax. What he does reject, on empirical grounds, is a proposition drawn from it: that the syntax of a language can, and should, be so constructed that the semantic representation of each sentence is given in the part of its structural description which reflects the 'deep structure' of the sentence.

sentence, then the paradigmatic contrasts allowed by those constraints. The first capacity is the distinctively generative one, the second the distinctively differential.

Let us assume that in a given language the first capacity has been described in a generative syntax for that language. This would mean that step 3 in the syntagmatic strategy had been accomplished. Describing the second capacity mentioned, the differential one, would now mean taking step 4. How might this be done? To have a method for doing it would be to have a method for doing 'semantics', a way of assigning a meaning to any sentence in the language.

In order to consider this question I shall examine in some greater detail the sort of structural description which, as Chomsky foresees it, a generative syntax would assign to a sentence of the language; this, in sections 13 and 14. In section 15 I shall look at the psychological story which our model suggests about how speaker or hearer sees the meaning of a sentence. Finally, in section 16, I shall return to the question raised here and consider what sort of semantics the extended Saussurian model would put beside a generative syntax.

13. The structural description of a sentence gives in the first place what I shall call its 'categorial' structure—the sort of structure given by the traditional parsing procedure. To understand this is to recognise the noun phrases and verb phrases, to see which phrases are subjects, which predicates, and so on (see Chomsky 1965, 63–4). Different grammars provide this information in different ways—compare Chomsky, McCawley and Winograd—but the variation need not concern us.

When we know the categorial structure of a sentence—I mean, know it in practice, not necessarily in grammatical theory—we know the basic syntagmatic constraints operating in a sentence. It follows that we also know the basic paradigmatic contrasts which specify the meaning of any word in the sentence. Take the sentence 'John likes the office where he works'. Let us say that the categorial structure of the sentence requires a noun phrase as subject, a verb phrase, a noun phrase as object and a clause qualifying this object. Within these constraints most of the words are set up in contrast to a limited number of alternatives; we speak of 'words' for simplicity though in strictness we should probably speak of 'phrases'. 'John' might have been replaced by any proper name or definite description (e.g., 'the man'), 'likes' might have been replaced by any verb which can take a noun phrase as subject and a noun phrase as object, and so on. The exceptional word is 'where' which is absolutely required by the categorial structure : no other single word would fit.

The example brings out a point which is crucial for our analysis. This is that the concepts of constraint and contrast lead quickly to that of choice. The constraints define the contrasts against which any word is to be judged. The contrasts define the significance which the word has when considered as a choice made by the speaker. If they were not there to be seen by speaker and hearer then neither could see significance in the choice : the significance of the choice is differential.

In speaking of choice—and I do so on a Saussurian precedent —I do not suggest that the speaker deliberates about every word he utters : choice does not presuppose consideration. What it involves is the adoption of one among a number of alternatives where the subject is capable of giving a reason for his option—if only the reason that between certain alternatives there was no significant difference. In this sense the speaker's choice of any word—I leave out of account the categorially required word— can be seen as a choice from among the categorially allowable words, or at least as a choice from among the allowable words known to him.

What sort of a reason can be given for a word choice? In most cases the reason why the word is chosen is 'semantic' : most of the other words available would give the wrong idea about the message which the speaker wishes to communicate. 'John' is chosen because it is John who is in question, 'likes' because he does like his office, and so on. The speaker may have a further reason for choosing one rather than another of the semantically satisfactory words but this is not normally the case in ordinary conversation : in literature, particularly in poetry, it is the rule.

14. Apart from categorial structure the structural description of a sentence may give an account of its 'subcategorial' structure. The word is my own but the idea is derived from Chomsky's comments on what he calls the rules of subcategorisation (Chomsky 1965, 94–5, 152–3).

Syntax categorises words as nouns, verbs, adjectives, adverbs and so on. It may subcategorise them at two levels, by means of strict rules of subcategorisation or by means of 'selectional' rules. With its strict rules it subcategorises them by establishing for each word the categorial context in which it may occur. If the word is a verb these rules will say whether it may be followed by an adjective (like 'grow'), a that-clause (like 'believe'), or whatever. Selectional rules subcategorise in a distinct way by establishing for each word certain features of the words which may provide its context. Again, if the word is a verb, these rules will say whether it may take an inanimate subject, an abstract object, and so on.

To give a structural description of a sentence in terms of the categorisation of its constituent words is to show the general syntagmatic constraints on what may replace any word in the sentence. When we give the description in terms of the subcategorisation of the words do we make these constraints more specific? We do not when the subcategorisation is by strict rules : when we said that 'likes' in our example can only be replaced by a verb which can take a noun phrase as subject and a noun phrase as object, we already took for granted the strict subcategorisation of the word. We do make the syntagmatic constraints of a sentence more specific however, when we subcategorise the words by selectional rules. We say for example that 'likes' can only be replaced by a verb which can take an impersonal, relatively abstract, object like 'office'; we rule out—except in the metaphorical case discussed in section 52 below—alternatives like 'kicks', 'smokes' or 'seduces'. What I mean by the subcategorial structure of a sentence is the structure described when the words are selectionally subcategorised in a structural description of the sentence.

The status of selectional—or, as I shall also say, subcategorial —rules is matter for discussion. I am prepared to assume, with Chomsky, that they are best represented as rules of a generative syntax though the argument given in section 11 does not require this : it only requires that there be some rules which are of this kind, and categorial rules would satisfy the demand. I find unconvincing the suggestion that selectional rules reflect regularities in word combination which are best presented as matter for inductive learning, not essential matter in the learning of a language; the idea that a language might be mastered without mastery of these rules is unrealistic, if not incoherent (*pace* Cohen-Margalit; see section 53 below).

When we know the subcategorial structure of a sentence—again I mean, know it in practice, not necessarily in theory—we know the very specific syntagmatic constraints operating in the sentence; we know something more than that the knowledge of categorial structure alone gives us. The importance of this extra knowledge needs some emphasising.

Consider what it does for the hearer; a similar story can be told about the speaker. The significance of a semantically 'loaded' word is the significance which attaches to it by contrast with the other words that might have been used in its place. The fewer the number of words that might have replaced it the more perspicuous this significance. The effect of the specific subcategorial constraints in a sentence is precisely to make the significance of any particular word more perspicuous. The significance of 'likes' is that much clearer in our example because the alternatives allowed reduce to 'dislikes', 'loves', 'hates' and some few other words; also of course to the past or future tenses of 'likes' and the other words. With the number of alternatives reduced it is easier to grasp why precisely 'likes' should have been chosen by the speaker.

The point can be put in the terms of information theory (see Lyons 1969, 84–90). The main axiom of this theory is that the information carried by one signal in a string of signals—say a word in a sentence—is an inverse function of the probability of the signal occurring in that context. Thus if I say 'Good morning!' at breakfast I may mumble the first word without much being lost on you : in that context the word has high probability and therefore low information value. The effect of subcategorial constraints is to heighten the probability of one of the permissible words occurring at a particular place in a sentence. Between these words probabilities are distributed which, if they are measured in fractions, must add up to one—this represents the certainty that some word will occur. Thus any restriction on the number of words permissible raises the probability of occurrence attaching to each. This means that the word which does occur will not have as much information to carry as it might have had, it will not absorb so much of the hearer's attention. The meaning of the word will be that much more obvious.[9]

15. Our philosophical arguments, borrowed respectively from Saussure and Chomsky, require that we think of language as at once generative and differential. It is generative in enabling the speaker/hearer to see the (syntagmatic) constraints of any sentence, differential in enabling him to see each word against the (paradigmatic) contrasts allowed by those constraints. In the last two sections we have seen something of how these capacities work together. Have we now a plausible psychological story about what it is like for a speaker or hearer to understand a sentence?

Two things may make the story seem implausible. The first is that we may have made it seem that the speaker and hearer confront a categorial—and even subcategorial—structure as something given, something apparent before the choice or interpretation of words. This objection can be easily put aside. There is nothing to stop us saying—and everything to suggest—that the speaker chooses the structure of his sentence; presumably he does this 'simultaneously' with choosing the words of the sentence. All we have to maintain is that the choice of structure must be capable of being regarded as independent of the choice of words; this it is, since a structural description of a sentence need not mention any of the words used. On the other side there is nothing to stop us saying that the hearer settles on what the structure of a sentence is 'simultaneously' with settling on its interpretation. We can represent the process as a self-corrective one in which a structure is assigned, the interpretation it gives examined and the structure accepted only where the interpretation seems reasonable. It is heartening that a literary critic like William Empson describes the process of coming to grips with a poem in just such terms. 'We think not in words but in directed phrases, and yet in accepting a syntax there is a preliminary stage of uncertainty; the grammar may be of such and such a kind; the words are able to be connected in this way or that . . . a plausible grammar is picked up at the same time as the words

9. This effect can be achieved of course, not just by subcategorial constraints, but by 'constraints' imposed by common sense, for example, or common usage.

B

it orders, but with a probability attached to it, and the less probable alternatives, ready, if necessary, to take its place, are in some way present in the back of your mind' (Empson 304).

The second thing which may make our story seem implausible is that when we speak of a word being set off against its paradigmatic contrasts we suppose that the other words in the sentence are kept fixed. We speak of 'likes' in our example as being set off against 'dislikes', 'loves', 'hates' and such words, on the assumption that 'John . . . the office where he works' remains the frame. Without the assumption we could still speak of the categorial constraints on what may replace 'likes' but we would have to give up speaking of the subcategorial ones. Is the assumption realistic?

It can be made to seem so. Consider the situation of the hearer of the sentence which we took as our example; a corresponding story can be told about the speaker. When the hearer interprets the sentence uttered—that is, picks up the speaker's 'message'—he settles on one word as the 'focus' of the sentence (see Chomsky 1970, 199–205). He regards the sentence precisely as a choice of that word within the frame provided by the others. He must do this since the message of the sentence shifts as the focus moves to 'John', or 'likes', or 'office', or any of the semantically loaded words. The word which the speaker wishes to be taken as focus is indicated by the position or stress it receives, or by the situation of utterance, linguistic and extra-linguistic.

The necessity of focus dissipates the second implausibility in our story about sentence construction and interpretation. Focus once granted, it does seem reasonable to say that a hearer judges the focal word, not just against the paradigmatic contrasts allowed by the categorial structure, but against the fewer contrasts allowed by the subcategorial structure, the structure given by the frame of the other words in the sentence. One point must be added however to complicate the picture. This is that the hearer normally understands the significance of each 'sub-focal' word as well as of the focal word—though he may understand it with different degrees of awareness. To allow for this point we must suppose—to put the matter in a misleadingly psychological way—that the hearer considers each word in turn, within the frame provided by the others, before giving one word exclusive claim on the focal position. The supposition seems reasonable enough since we do often follow a procedure like this when we take time over the interpretation of a line of poetry. Perhaps the interpretation of a sentence in everyday life is an accelerated version of the procedure involved in interpreting poetry.

We begin to see that the Saussurian model of language gives the outline of a plausible psychological story about sentence construction and interpretation. Construction may be described in Saussure's term as 'articulation', the sorting out of parts—words—in a whole (S 10, 112–13). This, it now appears, must involve three choices: the choice of structure, categorial and even perhaps subcategorial, the choice of words, focal and sub-focal, and the choice of focus itself.

What corresponds to the 'articulation' of the speaker may be described as the 'attention' of the hearer (see Pettit). 'Attention' by its root means 'waiting' or, more literally, 'stretching out'; colloquially perhaps, 'hanging on'. To attend to what someone says is to wait or hang on his words. It presupposes some idea of what to expect in any word, but not an assured idea: to lack the first is to get lost, to fail to lack the second is to get bored. Knowledge of the categorial and subcategorial constraints on the words means in the normal case that this presupposed condition is realised and attention is possible. For any word in the speaker's sentence, most significantly for the focal word, it guarantees that the hearer will find it neither absolutely preposterous nor absolutely predictable. The word will be capable of engaging the hearer, being—in that context—familiar but interesting.

Corresponding to the three choices in the articulation of a sentence are three stages in attention to it. In the first, a categorial and subcategorial structure is assigned to the sentence—subject to confirmation by the acceptability of the interpretation it yields. In the second, each semantically loaded word is assigned focal position in a cycle of interpretations. In the third, one word is assigned this position, the other words being taken as sub-focal, and the sentence is given a single interpretation.[10]

16. We are now in a position to return to the question of section 12. Does Chomsky open the way to taking step 4 in the

10. What may be added is that the interpretations cyclically produced in the second stage will almost certainly be interactive: one will tend to correct another. Here perhaps we have a version of the 'hermeneutic circle'.

syntagmatic strategy for linguistics? Is there room within that strategy for a semantics as well as a syntax?

In section 12 I suggested that to be able to do semantics would be to be able to assign a meaning to every sentence in a language. On that characterisation semantics is a practical discipline, which may be more or less systematic, more or less methodical. It is clear from our discussion in the last three sections that the syntagmatic strategy does leave room for such a semantics: a 'differential' semantics, I will call it.

To do differential semantics is simply to adopt a particular method of interpreting a sentence, one which is suggested by our story about the ordinary hearer. Taking the sentence, you settle first on a view of its syntagmatic structure, categorial and, at least in outline, subcategorical; in doing this you may rely on syntactical intuition or on the explicit rules of a generative syntax. Next, you consider the differential significance of each word choice in the sentence, taking special account of the subcategorial constraints on alternatives; these are of special interest because they may be broken in exceptional, metaphorical usage (see section 52 below).[11] Finally, you settle on a focal word the significance of which gives the whole sentence an acceptable interpretation. If you fail to get an acceptable interpretation you start again at the beginning and try another view of the syntagmatic structure. The procedure is clear enough, except perhaps on one point. This is that when you take a view of the structure of the sentence I assume that among other things you decide on whether the speaker intends to make a statement, for example, or ask a question; such information is structural in the sense that it determines whether certain replacements are possible, whether they are in significant contrast with words actually used.

What interests someone doing differential semantics is the choices made by the speaker: mainly, the choices of words within the syntagmatic constraints set by the structure of the sentence. He may also look at the choice of structure, and the choice of

11. The significance of a word choice may be considered not just in semantic terms but in terms of general appropriateness: in a poem it may be considered, for example, in metrical and symbolic terms (see section 13 above and section 21 below). In the language of Frege ours is a semantics of 'tone' as well as of what is strictly 'sense'; also, as suggested at the end of this paragraph, it is a semantics of 'force', giving us access to the speech act intention (see Dummett 1–7, 84–8, 295–305).

focus—that is, focal position—since these are liable to be signifi-cant in certain contexts, particularly literary ones (see note 11). And, by natural extension of his method, he may sometimes look at the speaker's choice of style of delivery, or even context of delivery; this can reveal such detail as whether the utterance is sarcastic or serious.

We will wish to see differential semantics in the context of contemporary semantic approaches. It is broadly on the lines of the approach favoured by philosophers in the tradition of Austin and the later Wittgenstein (see Grice, Searle, Strawson). That approach, which we may call 'communication theory' insists that a sentence has meaning only because it can typically carry a communicative intention : roughly, the intention of a speaker to get his audience to see that he believes or wants something, for example, an intention which he makes no secret of expecting to be fulfilled simply by being recognised (see Grice). Differential semantics takes the point, directing attention to those features in a sentence which indicate the intentions of the speaker. The features are the factors imputable to choice : the words, the structure, the focus, and the style and setting.

Differential semantics is out of line with the major contem-porary alternative to communication theory; this we could call deep structure will be common to a number of sentences which any sentence will have a deep structure to be described by one (base) set of syntactical rules and a surface structure derivable from the deep one by another (transformational) set of rules; the deep structure will be common to a number of sentences which differ on the surface, and those sentences will have roughly the same meaning. The assumption leads naturally to a conception of semantics as dealing with deep structure. Semantics comes to be thought of as providing a 'semantic representation' of the deep structure, a representation under which the meaning is un-ambiguous and unmistakeable : the information relevant to determining the meaning is systematically displayed in the representation.

Deep structure theory has led to different styles of semantics. In one school, historically closest to Chomsky, semantics appears as an addendum to syntax which serves to map deep structures on to semantic representations (see Katz/Fodor, Katz; also Bierwisch and Weinreich). In another school it disappears in syntax, the deep structure of a sentence coming to be considered precisely as its semantic representation (see note 8). With this latter move, the base rules of syntax naturally come to be compared with the rules whereby logic might assign to a sentence its logical form : for the notion of a semantic representation is very close to that of logical form. Thus we find a *detente* between linguistics and logic and, more particularly, the attempt to extend the semantics of formal systems to natural language. Formal semantics, as it is called, would track down the 'atomic' sentences whose truth conditions—the only aspect of meaning considered relevant—are derivable from the extensions of their predicates, and try to formulate rules for revealing the truth conditions of 'complex' sentences in terms of the truth conditions of atomic ones (see Davidson, Tarski, Wallace; also Lewis, Montague). It would put sentences in logical form, or semantic representation, and also give a formal account of their meaning.

In espousing differential semantics I do not mean to deny validity or interest to a programme like that of formal semantics. The programme does make the controversial assumption that knowing the truth conditions of a sentence can be knowing its meaning (see Vermazen). And it does fail conspicuously to explain how the predicates of atomic sentences come to be given extensions (see Jardine). However it promises something of substantial interest : a systematic account of the effect on truth conditions of operators which form complex sentences : that is, operators like the sentential connectives ('and', 'or', 'if . . . then'), the quantifiers ('all', 'some') and perhaps modal operators ('It is possible that . . .', 'It is certain that . . .').

Espousing differential semantics only means believing that there is more to be said about the meaning of a sentence than is said in formal semantics, or in any such programme, and that keeping this more in mind leads to a different approach to the interpretation of the sentence. The approach has the disadvantage of constituting a concrete practice of interpretation, not a programme of theoretical interest. But, against that, it has the advantage of inspiring confidence. In taking it we do not have to rely on the possibility of a syntax assigning a deep structure to every sentence; we only require a grasp of the surface structure, and that grasp need only be intuitive. And, secondly, we can be sure in taking it that we will not be concentrated on just one aspect of a sentence's meaning such as its truth conditions or, to put it more fully, the intention of the speaker to communicate his belief that the truth conditions have been fulfilled.

To conclude this chapter : we saw in section 7 that the Saussurian model of language could be applied, with greater or lesser modification, in either of two ways—within a paradigmatic strategy, or within a syntagmatic one. The main reward of a paradigmatic strategy is a structural phonology of the sort proposed by Jakobson. The main reward of a syntagmatic strategy is a generative syntax like that put forward by Chomsky. But this second strategy, we can now see, also shows us the way to a differential semantics. Thus, there are three ways in which someone who is extending the Saussurian model beyond language may think of using it. He may look in the area of his interest for a discipline analogous to structural phonology, generative syntax or differential semantics. We shall come across all three uses of the model in our discussion of its range.

BIBLIOGRAPHICAL REFERENCES TO I

B. Berlin and P. Kay, *Basic Colour Terms,* Berkeley : University of California Press, 1969.

M. Bierwisch, 'Problems of Semantic Representations', *Foundations of Language* 5, 1969.

N. Chomsky, 'Review of Skinner, *Verbal Behaviour*' (1959) in Fodor and Katz, *Aspects of the Theory of Syntax,* Cambridge, Mass. : MIT Press, 1965.
>'The Current scene in Linguistics' (1966) in D. A. Reibel and S. A. Schane, ed., *Modern Studies in English,* Englewood Cliffs, N.J. : Prentice-Hall, 1969.
>'Deep Structure, Surface Structure and Semantic Interpretation' (1970) in Steinberg and Jacobovits (see below).

L. J. Cohen and A. Margalit, 'The Role of Inductive Reasoning in the Interpretation of Metaphor' in Harman and Davidson (see below).

D. Davidson, 'Truth and Meaning', *Synthèse* 17, 1967.

O. Ducrot and T. Todorov, *Dictionnaire encyclopédique des sciences du Langage,* Paris : Seuil 1972.

M. Dummett, *Frege,* London : Duckworth, 1973.

W. Empson, *Seven Types of Ambiguity,* Cambridge University Press, 1930.

J. A. Fodor and J. J. Katz, ed., *The Structure of Language,* Englewood Cliffs, N.J. : Prentice-Hall, 1964.

R. Godel, *Les Sources Manuscrites du Cours de Linguistique Générale,* Paris : Minard, 1957.

W. H. Goodenough, 'Componential Analysis and the Study of Meaning', *Language* 32, 1956.

G. R. Grice, 'Meaning', *Philosophical Review* 66, 1957.
>'Utterer's Meaning, Sentence-Meaning and Word-Meaning', *Foundations of Language* 4, 1968.
>'Utterer's Meaning and Intentions', *Philosophical Review* 78, 1969.

G. Harman and D. Davidson, ed., *The Semantics of Natural Language,* Dordrecht : Reidel, 1972.

L. Hjelmslev, *Prolegomena to a Theory of Language,* Bloomington, Indiana : Indiana University Press, 1953.

P. Ivic, 'Roman Jakobson and the Growth of Phonology', *Linguistics* 18, 1965.

R. Jakobson, *Selected Writings I : Phonological Studies,* The Hague : Mouton, 1962.

N. Jardine, 'Model Theoretic Semantics and Natural Language', in E. Keenan, ed., *Formal Semantics of Natural Language,* Cambridge University Press, 1975.

J. J. Katz, *Semantic Theory,* New York : Harper and Row, 1972.

J. J. Katz and J. A. Fodor, 'The Structure of a Semantic Theory' in Fodor and Katz (see above).

J. Kramsky, *The Phonome,* Munich : Wilhelm Verlag, 1974.

G. Lepschy, *A Survey of Structural Linguistics,* London : Faber, 1970.

D. Lewis, 'General Semantics' in Harman and Davidson (see above).

J. Lyons, *Structural Semantics,* Oxford : Blackwell, 1963.
> *Introduction to Theoretical Linguistics,* Cambridge University Press, 1969.

J. D. McCawley, 'Where do Noun Phrases Come From?' (1970) in Steinberg and Jacobovits (see below).

A. Martinet, *Elements of General Linguistics,* London : Faber, 1964.

R. Montague, *Formal Philosophy,* London : Yale University Press, 1974.

P. Pettit, 'For Structuralism', *Atlantis* 4, September 1972.

F. de Saussure, *Course in General Linguistics,* London : McGraw Hill, 1966.

H. W. Scheffler and F. G. Lounsbury, *A Study in Structural Semantics,* Englewood Cliffs, N.J. : Prentice-Hall, 1971.

J. R. Searle, *Speech Acts,* Cambridge University Press, 1969.

P. A. Seuren, ed., *Semantic Syntax,* Oxford University Press, 1974.

N. C. W. Spence, 'A Hardy Perennial', *Archivum Linguisticum* 9, 1957.

D. Steinberg and L. Jacobovits, ed., *Semantics: An Interdisciplinary Reader,* Cambridge University Press, 1970.

P. F. Strawson, 'Meaning and Truth', Inaugural Lecture, Oxford, 1969.

A. Tarski, 'The Concept of Truth in Formalized Languages' (1936) in *Logic, Semantics, Metamathematics,* Oxford, 1956.
> 'The Semantic Concept of Truth' (1944) in L. Linsky, ed., *Semantics and the Philosophy of Language,* Urbana : University of Illinois Press, 1952.

J. Trier, *Der Deutsche Wortschatz im Sinnbezirk des Verstandes*, Heidelberg, 1931.

N. S. Trubetzkoy, *Grundzüge der Phonologie*, Göttingen, 1958.

B. Vermazen, 'Semantics and Semantics', *Foundations of Language* 7, 1971.

J. Wallace, 'On the Frame of Reference' in Harman and Davidson (see above).

U. Weinreich, 'Explorations in Semantic Theory' in T. A. Sebeck, ed., *Current Trends in Linguistics III*, The Hague: Mouton, 1966.

T. Winograd, *Understanding Natural Language*, Edinburgh University Press, 1972.

L. Wittgenstein, *Philosophical Investigations*, Oxford: Blackwell, 1967.

II

The Range of the Model

17. *'A science that studies the life of signs within society* is conceivable; it would be a part of social psychology and consequently of general psychology; I shall call it *semiology* (from the Greek *semeîon* "sign"). Semiology would show what constitutes signs, what laws govern them. Since the science does not yet exist, no one can say what it would be; but it has a right to existence, a place staked out in advance. Linguistics is only a part of the general science of semiology; the laws discovered by semiology will be applicable to linguistics, and the latter will circumscribe a well-defined area within the mass of anthropological facts' (Saussure 16—cited above in I). This definition may stand, with one proviso : that semiology or 'semiotics' is also allowed to cover certain forms of artistic analysis; these can scarcely be regarded as a part of social or general psychology.

Semiology is the general science that would come of treating all 'sign-systems' in the way linguistics treats language. Structuralism is the movement of thought which presses and formulates the case for semiology, usually at a conceptual level but also in attempts at empirical analysis. Roughly speaking, the terms are interchangeable. It should be noticed that I give quite a specific sense to 'structuralism' : unlike some commentators, I do not take it to embrace every science, even every human science, which claims to investigate 'structures' (*pace* Piaget, and Boudon).

I am concerned with structuralism mainly at the conceptual level. What I want to examine is the conceptual guidance which it is capable of providing for non-linguistic semiology. Structuralism borrows the linguistic model of language and tries to fit this, in one way or another, to non-linguistic areas; the idea is that the model should suggest lines of empirical analysis. I want to examine the different ways in which the linguistic model can be fitted to other areas, and the grounds on which the fitting can be defended.

As a conceptual argument structuralism corresponds to the philosophical component in linguistics : it is a general characterisation of an object or objects of analysis, which provides guidance for empirical inquiry. This guidance however may be actual or after the fact. It may serve actually to stimulate empirical work; or it may serve after the fact to interpret empirical work already done. Thus it is intelligible that structuralism, as we shall find, is at once a manifesto for semiological analyses and a review of existing analyses—implicitly semiological ones.

18. In the conceptual characterisation which structural linguistics gives of language two elements stand out : mechanism and meaning. By that characterisation language is a mechanism —as indeed Saussure had emphasised—whereby meaning is produced : the meaning of words and the meaning of sentences. In those areas to which structuralism tries to extend the linguistic model we find the two elements recurring. They are all areas in which meaning is produced and in all of them something like the linguistic mechanism is assumed to operate.

Meaning needs some discussion, particularly as it arises in language. Speech acts, the exercises of language, are meaningful in the sense that in performing them people intend to communicate certain things. Sentences are meaningful in the sense that they enable people to perform the speech acts by which they communicate. Words are meaningful in the sense that a change of word may cause a change of sentence and a change in what the speaker communicates in his act of using that sentence.

The meaning of the speech act may be taken as the intention of the speaker to communicate that he believes a certain state of affairs to be so—if it is a statement—that he wants it to be made so—if it is a command—and so on. To grasp this intention as audience is to see the meaning of what the speaker is saying, what he means by his utterance.

The meaning of a sentence is closely related to the meaning of a speech act. In section 15 we saw that any sentence can carry different messages, according to the choice of focal word. When a sentence is used in a speech act one of the things the speaker does is choose a particular word as focal. The meaning of the speech act—the intention it exhibits—can be taken as the message which the sentence carries in this particular use. Correlatively, the meaning of the sentence can be taken as the set of possible speech act intentions which it can be used to exhibit.

The affinity between speech act meaning and sentence meaning is that each relates to a state of mind which it exhibits or can exhibit: the speaker's intention. The meaning of a word must be contrasted with meaning in this sense. The meaning of a word is sometimes taken, it is true, to involve a state of mind—an idea—and, more or less directly, a state of things with which the idea is connected—an object or event for example. This however is the nominalist mistake parodied by Wittgenstein. 'You say: the point isn't the word, but its meaning, and you think of the meaning as a thing of the same kind as the word, though also different from the word. Here the word, there the meaning. The money and the cow you can buy with it' (Wittgenstein 49—cited above in I).

Wittgenstein's reaction was to say that the meaning of a word is simply the use that can be made of it. The distinction between sentences and words which forces a distinction between the senses in which they have meaning is that if we *use* words, we *make* sentences (see Ryle). In performing speech acts we make sentences, we construct them as part of the performance—*de novo,* or relatively so. In making sentences we use words, we avail of a ready-made stock of them. The meaning of the sentence can be assimilated to the meaning of a speech act, but the meaning of a word is something apart. It is the capacity of the word to be used in a sentence and make a difference there—syntagmatically, by contrast with other word-categories or sub-categories, and paradigmatically by contrast with syntagmatic alternatives. Less ponderously, it is the capacity of the word to do some work. Nominalism is led away from this simple insight by the fact that the work which some words do is to secure a reference to a state of affairs—work they sometimes do in single-word sentences like 'Fire!'

19.   All intentional human acts are like speech acts in exhibiting states of mind: my behaviour with the spade may be unorthodox and my ultimate purposes obscure but it will be clear at least that I want to dig the garden. All such acts are, in a basic sense,

meaningful. Semiology however is not concerned with all of them. The acts on which it focuses are those that involve cultural constructions in the way that speech acts involve sentences. These constructions acquire meaning in the same way that sentences acquire meaning and they form the real objects of semiological analyses; it deals with them as linguistics deals with sentences.

Some preliminary examples are necessary. My dressing up for a day at the races is meaningful like any other intentional action : its meaning is a state of mind, my intention, and this is clearly revealed in what I do. The act is distinctive in this respect : its performance involves a cultural construction—the outfit of clothes which I choose, more or less inventively. This outfit corresponds to the sentence. A similar action is exemplified by my having a light snack. This is meaningful in the ordinary intentional sense but also involves a cultural construction : here it is the set of dishes, the menu, that I choose.

It is important at the outset to notice one disanalogy between speech acts and acts of this kind. This is that semiological acts are not generally acts of communication. An act of communication, I will say, must satisfy this requirement (among others) : that its desired effect E is achieved by the recognition on the part of an audience that E, precisely, is the effect which the agent intends (see Grice, Searle—cited above in I). Say that the effect which I seek in telling you something is to have you see what I believe; this, perhaps, in the hope that you will believe it too. If I achieve the effect it will be because you recognise that this is precisely the effect which I intend. Thus the act of telling you something satisfies our requirement for communication acts. The same cannot be said for the acts of dressing up or having a light snack. The desired effects of such acts are not ones achieved by the recognition on the part of an audience of what they are. I fail to tell you something if you do not recognise what effect I intend. I can dress up or have a light snack whether or not you, or any others, recognise what I am after.

The crucial analogy between speech acts and other semiological acts is not that they are both communicative but that they both involve cultural forms of realisation—in the one case sentences, in the other the constructions mentioned (contrast Eco 61; also Ducrot/Todorov 122—cited above in I). Here the word 'mechanism' rejoins 'meaning'. In semiological acts meaning is the product of mechanism. More specifically, it is the product of a mechanism of articulation which operates like language on a syntagmatic and paradigmatic axis : this at least is the structuralist postulate.

The postulate does seem a reasonable one. There is evidence of a mechanism of articulation at work in the two examples given—as if there were a 'language' of fashion and a 'language' of cuisine. Articulation means the sorting out of parts in a whole, elements in a string—under syntagmatic constraints and out of consideration for paradigmatic constrasts. Certainly there is a sorting out of elements both in dressing up and in having a light snack : in the one case items of clothing are sorted out to form a particular outfit, in the other dishes are sorted out to form a particular menu. Furthermore this sorting out seems to operate on a syntagmatic and paradigmatic axis, in accordance with the rules of fashion and cuisine. There are syntagmatic constraints which ensure that certain dishes and certain items of clothing do not go together, at least in a certain order. There are paradigmatic contrasts which ensure that the contribution of any particular element to the string can be easily measured : you replace the element with an alternative allowed by the general rules and see what happens. The replacement in the outfit example will change the style of dressing up or it will change dressing up into something else—say, dressing casually.

20.   When structuralists begin to describe fashion and cuisine on the model of language, and outfits and menus on the model of sentences, one feels like protesting : the procedure seems strained, even a little absurd. The protest is somewhat premature. The structuralist can put a fair argument—a conceptual one— that it is necessary to invoke something like a mechanism of articulation to explain how it is possible for fashion and cuisine to produce such a varied number of 'strings', each distinctive in meaning. The argument amounts to saying that there must at least be differential structure in the 'languages' of fashion and cuisine. The point of the argument however is to set up fashion and cuisine for semiological investigation. What the structuralist can claim with absolute justification is that it is too early to protest against his use of the linguistic model in any area if there has not been consideration of the possibilities which it opens for

empirical inquiry. The point is not just that the model meets a conceptual requirement but also that it serves an empirical function.

Despite this reply structuralism in France has had to face a storm of protest on so-called 'grounds of principle' against the 'dehumanisation' of man's activity. Unfortunately for structuralism this dehumanisation has been proclaimed victoriously by Michel Foucault in his very personal reading of the history of ideas : he argues that with the semiological sciences the concept of the human subject has vanished from our *Weltanschauung* (see Foucault 1966—cited below in III). With equal relish Claude Lévi-Strauss boasts of the dehumanisation which he thinks—not unjustly—that his particular structuralism involves. He accepts Ricoeur's characterisation of the philosophy presupposed in his approach as a Kantian philosophy without a subject (see Lévi-Strauss 1964, 11—cited below in III).

French critics, mainly phenomenologists, have seized on such extreme anti-personalist statements in their criticism of structuralism (see for example Dufrenne) but their position is defined in equally extreme terms. The basic phenomenological concept is that of intentionality (see Pettit 1969). Phenomenologists argue that every conscious act involves 'intentionality', that in every such act—one of perception, for instance, imagination or desire—the individual subject 'constitutes' the object with which he is concerned. Take an object of preception like a hat or a flower. It is of the essence of such an object that it is something which continues as the same thing through a period of time, occupies to the exclusion of other things a portion of space and belongs to a certain category and class. The phenomenological argument is, roughly, that the object is seen as an object continuing in time because the individual who perceives it associates the object perceived with an object remembered; it is seen as an object occupying space because he assumes that it has other profiles than that which he registers at any moment; it is seen as an object of a certain category and class because he presents it to himself as similar to a range of other objects.

The doctrine that the individual 'intentionally' constitutes the objects of his consciousness is often softened by the insistence that he is influenced by his culture, his 'life-world', in how he constitutes them so that he inevitably follows the same lines as other people (see Pettit 1975). In existentialist writings the harder conclusion is drawn that the individual is responsible for how he constitutes the 'world'. He is said to be responsible for what 'meaning' he gives to things and therefore what meaning he gives to the words in which he describes them (see Sartre; also Pettit 1968).

This is individualism with a vengeance, a defence of the 'person' which easily matches in extremeness the structuralist attack on him. The structuralist has an easy time with it because the view of words suggested misses the fact that language—a social institution—is needed to give words meaning; existentialism involves something like nominalism. I do not have discretion over what my words will mean and, so long as I speak the common language, I do not decide on the 'meaning' of the things I describe with them. My 'world' therefore is a social construct, not my personal creation.

Much of the structuralist debate in France has been a debate on the issue with phenomenology: uselessly, since the positions defended are so extreme and the argument joined so abstract. A good example of the extravagance of the debate is the claim defended out of structuralist sympathies by Jacques Derrida, that phenomenology is only the last expression of a mistake traditional in Western metaphysics: 'logocentrism' (see Derrida 1967a, 1967b, 1968). This is the mistake of not seeing that meaning—the meaning of words and, something scarcely distinguished by Derrida, the 'meaning' words give to things—is due to the arbitrary play of contrasts, a play in which the individual joins both as writer and reader—the roles are not separate. Logocentrism suggests that there is an absolute order, in the mind or in reality, which gives rise to meaning, it does not see that this play is without beginning and without end, aimless. Derrida hardly conciliates the opposition when he upstages existentialism and calls, as response, for a Nietzschean joy in the caprice of things (see also Barthes 1973, Deleuze).

21.   This debate apart, the question is, what range is there for the structuralist use of the linguistic model. Rom Harré distinguishes between two types of model which science uses and the distinction will be useful in this discussion (Harré 174; see also Harré cited below in IV). A model may be a 'homeomorph' or a

'paramorph'. In the first case the subject of the model is also the source : the doll is a model of a baby and is also modelled on a baby. In the second case subject and source differ : the double helix is a model of the DNA molecule but is modelled on a simple mechanical structure.

In the first plausible opening for structuralism and semiology the linguistic model is charged with working as a homeomorph. This is in the analysis of stylistic devices, particularly in poetry. Here the linguistic model of language is used to provide a model of, precisely, language. More specifically, the account of words and sentences given within the model is applied to the words and sentences which stylistics seeks to examine. Every sentence comes out as articulated : as we would say, it is the result of a choice of structure, a choice of words and a choice of focus. The stylistician will seek a reason for every choice represented in the sentences with which he is dealing : Why this syntactic structuring? Why this or that word? Why this focus? He will not be primarily concerned with semantic answers : indeed his questions presuppose that the semantic purposes could have been fulfilled in other ways. What he is after is a specific explanation of every linguistic choice in the text—in terms of stylistic devices, in terms of tacit symbolism, and so on.

Stylistics is bound to be an intrinsic part of any structuralist project. If it has not received very much emphasis in recent French writing this is because no case needs to be made for it : stylistics is an accepted part of twentieth-century literary analysis (see Babb, Hough, Sebeok). The popularity of stylistics is not surprising in view of the emphasis of the 'new criticism', after I. A. Richards and William Empson, on attention to the text of a poem. Empson's work on ambiguity effects in poetry is a good example of stylistic analysis though the semantics which it involves is not explicitly formulated (see Empson—cited above in I).

This first use of the linguistic model cannot well be faulted but it is in place to remark on one danger. To do an analysis of a short text is to show the reason, ideally, for every choice in the text. But what is to count as a choice, and what not? The poet chooses a particular word for its metrical effect, we naturally suppose, but does he also choose it for the effect of its initial letter? Where we have evidence of the poet's explicit intentions we will answer 'yes', but we may still wish to answer 'yes' where we lack this evidence or even where the evidence goes against us : this, because we may wish to say that the choice was a tacit one, the significance of the initial letter of the word bearing in on the poet only unconsciously. This feature of analysis creates a danger for the analyst. He may be tempted to regard every pattern or device he notices in the text—and every effect he can trace to it—as significant, as a matter of choice. Thus he may be led into an arbitrary and uninteresting 'pattern-picking'. It is difficult not to conclude that Jakobson and Lévi-Strauss, for example, are led into such pattern-picking in their analysis of Baudelaire's *Les Chats* (see Jakobson, Lévi-Strauss; also, for criticism, Riffaterre).

What principle can we invoke to control stylistic analysis, to confine it to significant patterns and effects? The principle I would like to suggest has been formulated by John Rawls in quite another context and named the 'principle of reflective equilibrium' (see Rawls 20–21, 48–51; also Pettit 1974). The stylistic analysis of a poem, the account of significant patterns in the poem and their effects, must be in equilibrium with our intuitive sense of what effects matter in that poem and in poems of its sort. This, generally : in a limited number of cases the analysis may be allowed, Socratically, to revise our intuitions. The equilibrium is reflective in the sense that the analysis brings attention to bear on the grounds of our intuitions and should enable us to understand them better. If it were used to control stylistic analysis the principle of reflective equilibrium would force the analysis to respect the general psychology of a poem's audience. This is certainly reasonable, especially in view of the fact that the analysis is still allowed to revise that psychology in some measure.

The argument for imposing the principle of reflective equilibrium on stylistic analysis is not just that it gives as good a way as any for drawing the line between significant analysis and pattern-picking. The principle also has the advantage of suggesting a nice formulation of the point of such analysis. It presents the analysis as the attempt to explain those effects on which we do—or, in some cases, should—intuitively rely in reading and appreciating a poem. It is hard to quarrel with this account of stylistic analysis. Indeed, the account seems to sum up the point of any semiological analysis, even analysis involving more than a homeomorphic use of the linguistic model. This we shall see in time.

22.   The real test case of a structuralist enterprise is the use of the linguistic model as a paramorph. In this case it is not sentences themselves which are treated on the linguistic model of the sentence but things like sentences—menus and outfits for instance. There are three areas where entities are to be found which resemble sentences in the required way : they have meaning of such a kind that they can exhibit certain states of mind and they produce this meaning by something like a mechanism of articulation. The areas are : the literary arts for which stylistics does not cater adequately—the narrative, the dramatic and the cinematic; the non-literary arts such as music, architecture and painting; and the customary arts, as I shall call them—fashion, cuisine, and so on (for examples of analysis see the standard anthologies—Ehrmann, De George, Lane, Mackay/Donato, and Robey).

Among the literary arts I intend to discuss the possibility of providing a semiological analysis of narrative. This is the task which has received most attention among French structuralists and I shall make frequent reference to their work, primarily that of Roland Barthes and Tzvetan Todorov. In a larger study reference might have been made to work in other schools, for example the work of the Russian Formalists (see Bann/Bowlt and Erlich). Also separate attention might have been given to the related problems of analysing drama and cinema semiologically (see, on cinema, Metz).

The analysis of the narrative text—the epic, novel, short story, folk tale or myth—seems at first sight to use the linguistic model as a homeomorph. After all the text is linguistic itself. It is stylistics however which concerns itself with the text in its specifically linguistic aspect. What narrative analysis takes up is the subject-matter of the text—the actions, the characters, the story, the themes, and so on. This subject-matter—I shall say simply, the text—is constructed out of language but constitutes something non-linguistic itself.

Structuralism suggests that the narrative text is analogous to the sentence on two counts. First, the text is a meaningful whole which may be presumed to express the state of mind of a writer in the way a sentence expresses the state of mind of a speaker. Its meaning is more than what is grasped just by understanding the individual sentences in which the text consists : I may understand these and miss the meaning of the whole. What the text expresses therefore is more than what the sentences individually express. Secondly, the text shows evidence of being articulated out of parts in the way a sentence is articulated out of words. It is a compound of events which fall together to make up a story and to manifest characters in action.

The central structuralist argument about narrative is that, just as in a sentence, it is the more or less mechanical articulation of the text which produces its meaning. There are two premises to the argument. The first is that the meaning of the text is dependent on the meaning of its parts in the sense that if the meaning of a part changes then so, in some measure, does the meaning of the whole. The other premise is that the meaning of every part, the meaning of every event involved in the text, is determined by the events which might have occurred in place of it without making nonsense of the whole : the significance of the event appears only against the background contrast of alternatives. These premises put the narrative text on a footing with the sentence because the meaning of a sentence is also dependent on the meaning of its parts—the words in the sentence—and the meaning of every word is determined by the contrast with possible replacements. They suggest the conclusion that the text produces its meaning precisely by being articulated out of parts—within syntagmatic constraints, with regard for paradigmatic contrasts. In section 24 I accept the argument leading to this conclusion, but in a form in which the conclusion is spelled out more clearly.

23. His central argument gets the structuralist under way because it implies that he should treat the narrative text in the way the linguist treats the sentence. But immediately he faces an alternative : to take an informal differential semantics as his model and to go for what I shall call 'straight' analysis of particular texts or to be systematic in his approach and to look for something like Chomsky's grammar or Jakobson's phonology. In some recent structuralist writing, particularly that of the *Tel Quel* group, the first option has become the dominant one (see *Tel*

Quel). What it means is that the analyst approaches his text or set of texts—an *oeuvre* or a genre—content with this idea : that the meaning here, the meaning that I grasp in reading the text, is the result of the mechanism of articulation and will be explained by the patterns of articulation in the text. This structuralist looks in a relatively unsystematic way for such patterns or devices and usually ends by arguing for the dominance of one or two distinctive examples.

The kinds of straight analysis possible however vary greatly among themselves. This can be seen if we look at some examples in explicitly structuralist writing of what I should call straight analysis. A first example is Barthes's analysis of Racine's plays. He settles on a pattern in the stories of those plays which is supposed to account for their distinctive meaning or effect. The pattern is simply described : 'A has full power over B. A loves B who does not love him' (Barthes 1963, 35). A second example of straight analysis is Todorov's outline analysis of Henry James's early stories. The pattern which he takes to be crucial in these stories is a 'figure' which he claims to find at different levels of the texts, in story, characterisation, even linguistic style. 'The secret of James's tales is . . . [the] existence of an essential secret, of something which is not named, of an absent, overwhelming force which puts the whole machinery of the narrative into motion' (Todorov 1973, 75). A third, and final, example of what I would regard as straight analysis is an analysis of Joyce's *Finnegan's Wake* by Stephen Heath, a prominent English recruit to the *Tel Quel* group. He argues that the dominant patterns in the *Wake* are those which allow language to be seen for what it is, the play of effects of contrast : 'its negation is the refusal of compromise and the acceptance of the game of language; its anti-language is not the disappearance of language but its dramatic presentation' (Heath 32).

There can be no objection to straight analysis though the extent to which it depends on the linguistic model may be questioned. The striking thing about the analysis is that it does not identify in narrative texts anything that might count as the 'language' of narratives : if the texts are 'sentences' there is no 'language' to govern their construction. What the linguistic model does for this sort of analysis is a useful, but not a necessary, service. It enables the analysis to formulate its programme in an attractive and suggestive way, as the search for patterns which produce crucial narrative effects.

If straight analysis of narrative is unobjectionable however, it does involve a danger : the danger of uncontrolled analysis which also arises in the stylistic case. There has been a tendency in the *Tel Quel* group to argue that any devices and any patterns in a text may be taken as significant, and not just those with effects that would generally be regarded as worthy of notice. Thus it would be quite sensible to think of analysing a text as a play of anagrams, for example, and reading it accordingly. The *Tel Quel* fundamentalism on this point derives in part from Derrida's insistence that the play of contrasts in which language produces meaning is an arbitrary play of contrasts arbitrarily chosen; on the linguistic analogy, there is nothing wrong with writing or reading a text against a background of unconventional contrasts, giving it quite an unconventional meaning. It is difficult to argue against such fundamentalism. All one can say perhaps is that so long as reading is taken in its ordinary sense—and certainly this is the only sense in which its value is proven—analysis must be subject to the control of something like the principle of reflective equilibrium. To reject the control of that principle is to despise the general psychology of readers and drive literary analysis into the sheerest caprice.

24. The structuralist's first alternative, in discussing narrative, is this : straight analysis or a systematic approach. The systematic option which we must now consider leads to a second alternative : to go for a theory on the Chomsky model or to go for one on the Jakobson model. I shall describe this as the alternative of 'generative' and 'descriptive' theory.

In the analysis of narrative a generative theory would consist in a system of rules by means of which a structure—the syntagmatic structure, or part of it, which paradigmatic contrasts presuppose—could be assigned to any narrative text—or at least any one of a particular class of narrative texts. Barthes proposes such a theory in *Critique et Vérité*, a polemical essay of 1966, but never follows up the proposal; indeed he later rejects altogether the idea of a systematic theory of literature (Barthes 1971, 44–5). Julia Kristeva takes up the proposal in her early study on *Le Texte du Roman* and argues, not very convincingly, that it should be possible to formulate a theory which would assign plot structure to a novel; the structure she considers assigning is an abstract scheme of the action and does not carry immediate interest. Jonathan Culler also considers Barthes's proposal favourably in a recent argument for seeing literary theory on a generative model but he does not press his argument in detail (Culler 137–235). Finally something like Barthes's proposal is implied in the programme—by its nature extremely abstract—of certain German analysts for a grammar of narrative texts (*Poetics*).

Barthes follows Chomsky in his proposal. He assumes that the native reader is possessed of a distinctive literary competence by means of which he can recognise an 'acceptable' text and assign it a structure. The acceptable text is presumably the one which is coherent in the terms of some existing or conceivable genre, and which can be read consistently—can at least be given comparable interpretations—from reader to reader. The task which Barthes sets for literary theory is to model literary competence in a system of recursive rules which can be used to provide a structural description of a given text. 'The science of literature will have to show, not why such a meaning should be accepted, nor even why it has been accepted—that is still the task of the historian—but why it is *acceptable*—not in terms of philological rules of the letter but in terms of linguistic rules of the symbol' (Barthes 1966a, 58).

At the source of Barthes's proposal is a reading—a plausible reading, which I accept—of the central structuralist argument about narrative, the argument mentioned in section 22. The first premise of that argument was that the meaning of a text depends on the meaning of its parts, since a change of meaning of any part changes the meaning of the whole. Thus if a particular event is seen as a tragic finale, story-wise and character-wise as the price of the hero's credulity, it cannot be seen in any other way without the whole text being seen in some other way. The second premise of the argument was that the meaning of every part of the text, the meaning of every one of its constituent events, is determined by the events which might have taken its place without making nonsense of the text as a whole, the events against which it stands out in contrast. Thus the event mentioned is seen as a tragic finale by contrast with the events which might have given the story a happy ending. The conclusion of the argument in section 22 was simply that a text produces its meaning as a sentence does, by an articulation which sets up the appropriate contrasts for its different parts. Here we may spell this out in some greater detail.

Consider the text from the point of view of the reader; corresponding considerations can be offered from the point of view of the writer. What determines his view of the events which might have taken the place of any event he comes on in the text? Surely the fact that he projects a certain structure on the text: it is, let us say, a realistic novel in which he expects to find certain types of characters, in certain settings, involved in a story that will have a certain type of outcome. On first reading he will project this structure by anticipation, afterwards from memory. The structure puts limits on what can be expected to occur at any point in the text and so sets up the contrasts required to define the significance of the event that does in fact occur at that point. A plausible reading therefore of the conclusion of the argument in section 22 is that, just as with a sentence, a narrative text can be given meaning, can be interpreted, only when it is assigned a structure. This conclusion does not entail however, as Barthes would hold, that the reader who interprets a text is master of a generative grammar of narrative. This proposition follows only on the further premise that such structure can only be assigned generatively: that is, in the way represented by a generative grammar.

The premise is not a general truth—though categorical structure is assigned generatively to sentences—and it does not seem to hold in particular of narrative structure. If the assigning of structure is to be represented in a generative grammar then this condition at least must be fulfilled: that it is intuitively clear when a text has structure and when it fails to have structure, when it is allowable and when it is unallowable. The corresponding condition is met by sentences because his intuition tells the native speaker when a sentence is grammatical and when it is ungrammatical. The condition is not met by narrative texts for two reasons. First, there is no intuition by which a reader can definitely say that a text lacks structure and is unallowable. Second, and related to this, there is no single structure in virtue of which a text is allowable: most texts will have many structures

—given by plot development, character development or thematic development for example—by reference to which they can be read; and any text, one is tempted to add, will have some.

Structure, I want to say, is assigned to a narrative text as a *gestalt* perceived there, not on generative grounds. If we put a spread of dots on a blackboard, the eye will almost certainly see a pattern in them—one overall shape or a distribution of shapes. This is in accordance with the law of *prägnanz* discussed in Gestalt psychology : roughly, the law that in any set of data the mind sees a good form—one that is simple, continuous and bounded, for instance—and a comprehensive form—one that takes account of a high proportion of the data. 'The principle contends that organisation of a field tends to be as simple and clear as is compatible with the conditions given in each case' (Kohler 251).

This law operates in our perception of dots on a board but does not dominate that perception in the way a recursive procedure does : it often allows oscillation between two or three 'pregnant' forms and it never fails to present some form. It would seem to be a law of this kind that operates in our perception of structure in a narrative text. We can always opt as readers for one or another organisation of the text. And, unless we are very unimaginative, we rarely fail to put some organisation on it.

It is true that there is no merely natural text and no merely natural sense of pregnant form. The conventions of a period and a genre always serve to define what makes for such a form. However, these conventions can be acknowledged within a *gestalt* framework and described there. Certainly they need not press one to the conclusion that here we have rules which operate recursively. The idea of a genre and what it allows is too uncertain to justify trying to formulate recursive rules which might mirror these conventions.

25.   The alternative to generative theory was descriptive theory. This would take the paradigmatic approach of section 7 and try to characterise the elements of narrative in the terms required for their paradigmatic contrast, before trying to formulate syntagmatic constraints on how they combine. Here, as in generative theory, the goal of the structuralist is not just to analyse particular

texts or sets of texts but to offer an account of the 'language' of narrative. The 'language' which he now seeks is not a system of recursive rules but a set of elements in certain paradigmatic and syntagmatic relationships : something like Jakobson's phonemes.

There are two forms which a descriptive theory of narrative might take. It might approach the text as a set of characteristic events or it might approach it as a structure with a number of parameters; I shall speak in the first case of a 'material' theory, in the second of a 'formal'.

The formal theory would pick out certain general features of narrative which take different values from text to text and take them, with their concrete values, as the elements articulated in any text. Thus any text is presented as a combination of these elements, each of which has its significance defined by its contrast with the other possible values of the variable feature it represents. Suppose we took these as the crucial features of narrative : the setting, the characters and the story, the narrator's presentation, his perspective and his purpose. Each of these features is a variable with different possible values : the setting, the characters and the story can be historical or fictional, for example, and if fictional, realistic or non-realistic; the presentation can be detached or involved, focused on character or on story; the perspective can be past or present, internal or external, omniscient or partial; the purpose can be to entertain or to edify, to illustrate a theory or to explore new possibilities. A formal descriptive theory of narrative would take each variable as a cluster of paradigmatically related elements and try to work out the possibilities of combination among these elements.

The formal type of descriptive theory is represented in France by Todorov, who looks for a 'poetics' which would show how any narrative text is possible by showing what combination of formal features it represents. 'Poetics will not have for its task the correct description or interpretation of literary works of the past but the study of conditions which make possible the existence of these works' (Todorov 1967, 8). The conditions which are supposed to make possible the existence of any narrative work are defined in terms of its formal features : the work is possible because the combination of features which it represents is allowed within the 'language' of narrative. The goal of poetics is to give a systematic account of those conditions by working out all the legitimate combinations possible among the formal features of narrative.

Is formal theory in this sense a plausible idea? Well, it is certainly possible to set about deducing the mathematically possible combinations of narrative features; it will be more difficult to find grounds for saying that any of these is illegitimate but this problem we may leave aside. What is possible is not always interesting however, and it seems more than likely that such a deduction would have little interest. If the elements in a narrative text are described abstractly enough to present the text as one among a number of abstract possibilities, they will usually be described too abstractly to reflect the distinctive properties of the text. Thus the abstract deduction of poetics would amount to nothing more than a game, of little use in explaining what is distinctive about different texts, and of little intrinsic interest (see also section 59 below).

What presents itself as formal theory however may have a non-theoretical interest. To isolate the formal features of narrative, and plot the different values which they may assume, is to give oneself a set of categories for approaching the analysis and criticism of any particular text, or the comparative analysis of different texts. In a recent work this is the use which Todorov sees for poetics: it provides a scheme for criticism—and, we might add, comparison—but only a guiding scheme, since it may be revised on each occasion of use. 'Literary theory—poetics—provides criticism with instruments; yet criticism does not content itself with applying them in a servile fashion, but transforms them through contact with new material' (Todorov 1973, 73).

The other type of descriptive theory, which rivals the formal variety, would take the events in a text, not its formal features, as the elements of narrative. This 'material' theory would try to draw up an inventory of events characteristic of narrative texts and would seek to establish the paradigmatic and syntagmatic relations between them. As in the case of formal theory, it would strive to present any text as a concrete example of a combination allowed by the abstract 'language' of narrative elements.

In the very year in which he published his generative proposals Barthes, who is not a model of consistency in these matters, also put forward proposals for a material descriptive theory of narrative (see Barthes 1966b). Barthes builds his descriptive scheme around the concept of a 'function' which he takes from the pioneer formalist, Vladimir Propp. The function is the basic element of a text, consisting in a string of words of variable length, and constituting an event proper or the 'event' of a state : a trait of character, a type of situation, and so on. The function is bound syntagmatically in one or both of two types of relations with other functions : 'integrative' ones which make it significant in the picture of setting or character and 'distributional' relations which make it significant in the story told by the text; the distinction Barthes borrows from the French linguist, Emile Benveniste (see Benveniste, chapter X). Any analysis of a text should isolate and describe the functions, the pattern among their syntagmatic relations—integrative and distributional—and the definitive paradigmatic contrasts. Presumably a material theory—Barthes does not spell out the point—should display the abstract possibilities of combination among typical functions.

Barthes is only one of a number of French thinkers to have taken an interest in the idea of a material descriptive theory of narrative. Others include Claude Bremond and A. J. Greimas, whom Robert Scholes describes as the 'progeny of Propp' (Scholes 91). The description fits because Propp was the first to make thinkable the idea of a material theory. He took the body of Russian folk-tales and distinguished thirty-one functions which, at most, a tale might have : these range from the hero receiving an interdiction, to the hero leaving home, to the villain being punished (see Propp). These functions might be regarded as the elements of the folk-tales, defined in each case by the contrast with their opposites : the hero not receiving an interdiction, and so on. Propp argued for a minimal syntagmatic constraint on their combination : however many or few occurred in a text, they could occur only in the order in which they appeared in his general list. Propp opened up the possibility of describing the elements of narrative more generally and more elaborately, and of defining more complex constraints on their combination. This possibility is that which material theory of narrative explores.

Is the idea of such a theory plausible? The answer is the same as with formal theory. There seems to be nothing contradictory in the idea but neither does it command much interest. If a material theory describes the elements of narrative abstractly enough to make the deduction of abstract possibilities of combination possible then the chances are that it will have described them too abstractly to reflect the distinctive properties of different texts. On the other hand what presents itself as material theory or the outline of such theory may have considerable non-theoretical interest. It may offer a set of terms for approaching a certain sort of comparative analysis of texts. Indeed, on reflection, this is precisely what Propp's theory provides: its goal, after all, is the comparative analysis of Russian folk-tales, not an abstract theory in any strict sense of the term.

26.   In our discussion of each kind of descriptive theory of narrative we spoke of the analysis which such theory might make possible. The analysis in question is not 'straight' analysis but what I shall call 'systematic' analysis. It is systematic in availing of an organised set of categories to govern its approach.

The first structuralist alternative in tackling narrative was to pursue straight analysis or attempt a systematic approach. The second alternative, we can now see, is to pursue systematic analysis or attempt systematic theory. The alternative of generative and descriptive theory is really the third alternative which the structuralist faces.

Generative and descriptive theory take their cues respectively from Chomsky's grammar and Jakobson's phonology. Systematic analysis, like straight analysis, takes its cue from differential semantics. Its aim is to show the significance, within the limits set by the principle of reflective equilibrium, of every choice in a narrative text: the choice of structure, in its general outline and in particular features, and especially the choice of events to fill the structure. Systematic analysis is the parallel of stylistics when this tries to show the significance of every choice in a poem—not just semantic significance, but significance in metrical terms, in symbolic terms, and in terms of other poetic dimensions.

The functions in a text are what correspond to a poem's words: they are the parts articulated in the text. Systematic analysis should concern itself especially with the choices which these represent. If it has as its concern a particular sort of comparative analysis it may be content to be guided by inductive categories of the sort used by Propp for Russian folk-tales. Generally, it will draw on the sort of categories provided by a formal theory. As a list of such categories we suggested setting, characters, story, presentation, perspective and purpose. We might well use these terms to direct the analysis of a text or set of texts. Ideally, we would take the text function by function and show the significance of each element in terms of each factor: that is, its significance in serving the purpose of the author by presenting from a certain perspective the setting, characters or story of the text. We might want to get from this analysis a detailed characterisation of the text or a characterisation of the more general kind required for interesting comparison of different texts.

The best French example of systematic analysis is provided in a recent work, *S/Z*, by the protean Barthes (see Barthes 1970; for another good example see Genette 1973). Barthes is concerned in *S/Z* with a short story of Balzac. He divides the story into several hundred pieces of text. With each piece of text he asks a number of questions suggested by a list of factors—he calls them 'codes'—corresponding to our list of setting, characters, story and so on. Does the piece develop plot? If so, it is encoded 'proairetically'. Does it suggest or sustain a problem which the reader must hold in the back of his mind as he reads the text? If so, it is encoded 'hermeneutically'. Does it develop character? If so, it is encoded 'semically'. And so on. The terms are technical but the principle behind the approach is utterly uncomplex.

Systematic analysis, like straight analysis, requires nothing more by way of assumption than what the central structuralist argument provides under the reading which I gave it in section 24. This is the assumption that when a text is given an interpretation by a reader, it is given a structure that puts limits on what may replace any event in the text. What systematic analysis does is to show for each event the significance which it has, by contrast with possible replacements, in terms of setting, story, and other dimensions.

Systematic analysis is no more objectionable, and is probably more satisfying, than straight analysis. Is it any more distinctively structuralist? No, because it also fails to find a 'language' of narrative of which each text would be a 'sentence': it does not suppose that there is a given set of rules for the text to respect or a given set of elements for it to combine. What the linguistic model does in the case of systematic, as well as of straight, analysis is enable the analysis to give an attractive and suggestive formulation of its programme.

27.   It is now possible to present in a summary diagram the tree of options on which the structuralist analyst of narrative must decide his position—though he may also identify himself with other positions he has tried or hopes to try.

Figure 1

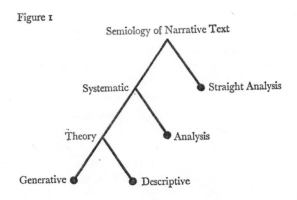

There are four terminal options represented on the tree: straight analysis, systematic analysis, generative theory and descriptive theory. The theoretical options are modelled respectively on Chomsky and Jakobson. They are purely programmatic, failing to promise success in the one case, interest in the other. The only realistic options are the analytic ones, both of which correspond in linguistics to an informal sort of differential semantics.

These options are also the least radical. They do not suggest very novel departures, not even departures of a distinctively structuralist stamp: this I have indicated already. The structuralist disappointment can be taken, not too mischievously, to have inspired two striking developments of the linguistic model. One is consummated in Lévi-Strauss and I discuss it in the next chapter. It is the attempt to reduce the patterns revealed in analysis of texts to transformations of a single formula or set of formulas. The other development I do not discuss as it has not yet been followed through. It is Kristeva's proposal for a 'semanalysis', an analysis on structuralist lines but to a sociological purpose; the aim would be to show what is characteristic about the 'signifying practices' of our society. 'If semanalysis concerns itself with the text, it is solely that it may provide itself with an object where the specificities of the signifying act are most clearly manifested' (Kristeva 1971, 9).

28. We have sketched the possible uses of the linguistic model in the study of one literary art—the narrative text. In the remaining sections of this chapter we must look at its possible uses in the examination of the non-literary arts and 'customary' arts. Our survey will be sketchy but it is necessary if we are to have a balanced idea of the range of the linguistic model.

By the non-literary arts I mean arts such as music, architecture, sculpture and painting. Among some French structuralists there is a resistance to taking these as proper objects of semiological investigation. Thus Ducrot and Todorov argue that because they are 'non-symbolic' they demand a different type of analysis (see Ducrot/Todorov—cited above in I). They mean that works of non-literary art do not refer to states of affairs and are not used to communicate the artist's wish to assert, question or prescribe states of affairs. This is no reason however to put non-literary arts beyond the range of the linguistic model. We saw in section 19 that behaviour to which the model is applied may not always be communicative in a strict sense.

The claim of the non-literary arts to be brought under the range of the linguistic model may be advanced first on the grounds that works of non-literary art resemble sentences in being meaningful and in being articulated out of parts. Thus, for example, a piece of music is meaningful in the sense that it serves to express the state of mind of the composer and, in complementary measure, that of the performer. It is articulated in the sense that it involves parts—these may be taken as chords, melodies, or whatever—which it sorts out under certain syntagmatic ordering constraints, with regard for certain paradigmatic contrasts.

The central argument for extending the linguistic model to music and the other non-literary arts—an argument which corresponds to that about narrative in section 22—is that a work of non-literary art produces its meaning precisely by the mechanical articulation of its parts. The first premise is that in any such work the meaning of the whole is dependent on the meaning of

C

the parts because if a part changes in its meaning the meaning of the whole changes too : if a chord in a piece of music changes key, a line in a painting balance, or an ornamental device in a building style, the deviation will reflect on the whole. The second premise of the argument is that the meaning of any part in a non-literary work of art is determined by the background contrast with what might have replaced it without making nonsense of the whole : the chord, the line or the ornamental device has its significance from its contrast with rival candidates for the place it occupies in the whole. The premises suggest that a work of non-literary art, like a sentence or a narrative, produces its meaning by having its parts articulated in such a way that each is set up against the appropriate contrasts.

We must now see what can be made of this central argument in working out different approaches to the analysis of non-literary art. What applications of the linguistic model does it license? The applications we shall consider are straight analysis and systematic analysis, generative theory and descriptive theory. To illustrate the different approaches we shall be drawing on theorists who are not explicitly structuralist but whose work can be considered in structuralist terms.

29.   The straight analysis of works of non-literary art is one approach which the structuralist argument of the last section would suggest. It is an unobjectionable approach and not an uninteresting one. Straight analysis would take any piece of music, any work of sculpture or architecture or any painting, and proceed, on a more or less intuitive basis, to explain how certain effects are produced in the work. The explanation would trace the effects to certain devices and patterns of articulation.

An example of straight analysis is the early Wölfflin's analysis of paintings (see Wölfflin). He takes a painting and, having settled on what he considers to be interesting effects, goes about trying to explain how those effects are produced. In his explanations he appeals, in a more or less *ad hoc* way, to plays of shadow and light, plays of colour and plays of line and balance.

Straight analysis of non-literary works of art does not depend intrinsically on the linguistic model but the model offers a suggestive way of formulating what it is after. It is worth mentioning a test that the model suggests, which may be used in analysis of a non-literary work, or indeed in analysis of a literary one. In linguistics the test is known as the 'commutation test' and was first formulated by Hjelmslev (see Hjelmslev—cited above in I; also Barthes 1964, 65). The test consists in replacing a word in a sentence and watching the effect on the whole of different replacements. It provides a rough index of the work done by the word in the sentence. In aesthetic analysis the test would consist in replacing—or imagining replacing—one or another element of the work of art so as to get an idea of the effects for which it is responsible. Abraham Moles actually proposes a technique of aesthetic analysis which can be seen as a version of the commutation test. 'One of the most general heuristic procedures of aesthetics, based on the materiality of the work of art, consists of progressively destroying the work by known, perceptible quantities, and in following the variations in aesthetic sensation, value, and knowledge as a function of this destruction' (Moles 201).

30. The other option to straight analysis, the systematic one, leads the structuralist to the alternative of theory and analysis. The theory option is closed because neither option on the theoretical alternative is very promising. Take the generative one first. Some analysts have drawn a parallel between genre in architecture—it might well have been genre in music or painting—and grammar in Chomsky's sense (see Portoghesi). There is some parallel but it can scarcely be pressed for theoretical purposes. The structure which I put on a piece of music, a work of architecture or a painting—the outline order within which I place and value this or that element of the work— is not a structure assignable by a set of recursive rules. This, for the same reasons given in the case of narrative : there is no intuitive criterion of structure firm enough to guide the application of such rules. Here again it appears that the subject assigns a structure or form to a work of art on a *gestalt* basis rather than by a generative procedure.

Descriptive theory is a more realistic option than generative but, just as in the case of narrative, is not a very interesting one. Norberg-Schulz, again in architecture, points to the possibility of such a theory when he tries to define the elements which any work of architecture would combine in a more or less distinctive way: 'the elements may be defined as "space-cells", "mass-forms" and "bounding-surfaces". Or the element can be a *gestalt* combining these aspects' (Norberg-Schulz 105). Definition of these elements suggests that the way is open for a 'poetics' of architecture in Todorov's sense of the term, a poetics which would 'derive' actual buildings and kinds of building as possible architectural combinations among others. It is significant that Norberg-Schulz does not explore the possibility of such a descriptive theory. The terms of the theory would be too abstract for it to link up tightly with actual works of architecture. The theory might be an enjoyable game but would have little explanatory interest.

31. The observation leads us back to the option for systematic analysis. This option is as unobjectionable as that for straight analysis. It does not involve the postulate of a 'language'—whether a system of rules or a set of predefined elements—of music, architecture, sculpture or painting, but avails of the linguistic model to help it in formulating its programme. The assumption it does make is that given by the central argument mentioned in section 28 : that the non-literary work of art, like a sentence, produces its meaning by the way in which it articulates its parts. This can now be taken to mean, as in the case of narrative, that the 'audience' of such a work projects a structure on it which defines the possible replacements for any element.

The assumption leads the systematic analysis to think of showing, for each element in a work of art, what alternatives are allowed by the projected structure and what significance it has by contrast with them. Systematic analysis corresponds to stylistics when the latter describes the significance of the words of a poem in semantic, metrical and symbolic terms, and to narrative analysis when it describes the significance of events in a text in terms of narrator's presentation, from a definite perspective and with a definite purpose, of setting, character or story. Systematic analysis of non-literary works of art must opt for a set of terms or categories reflecting the important features in the art in question and then pursue the description of individual works, part by part.

It is worth noting that the choice of theoretical terms to guide systematic analysis presents something of a problem in all of the non-literary arts. Traditionally, there have been two kinds of terms : the technical and the expressive. The analysis directed by technical terms is that which is popular among professionals. Examples are the analysis of music in terms of the variety of chords, phrasing, modulation and so on or the analysis of architecture by reference to characteristics of period and style (see for example Summerson). Such analysis is usually purely descriptive though there has been a tendency in analysis of music to look for a 'key' formula in every work. Thus 'motivic analysis' looks for a basic motif of which the work offers a series of trans-formations, 'linear analysis' looks for a cadential formula which the work delays and prolongs (see Rosen 33–42; also, on linear analysis, Salzer). These kinds of analysis leave much out of account—most notoriously, rhythmic pattern—and can be accused of giving only the appearance of rigour : you can always present two musical passages as transformationally related if you are generous enough with rules of transformation; you can always, with a little ingenuity, find a cadential formula 'hidden' in a musical score.

The criticism of descriptive technical analysis is precisely that it is technical and cannot hope to explain effects which are, after all, emotional. This criticism is the point of entry for expressive analysis which introduces terms from vocabularies of general evaluation and emotion to describe works of art. Thus every painting, building or piece of music becomes subtle or obvious, serene or tense, sad or jolly, light or serious, and so on. Expressive analysis does compensate for the academicism of technical but it has drawbacks of its own. The worst fault is that the terms it uses are necessarily vague and offer no hope of characterising artistic effects with any precision.

In recent years theorists have drawn on a third source of categories besides the technical and the expressive. The source is psychology of perception—mainly *gestalt* psychology, but also information theory. The main law of *gestalt* psychology, the law of *prägnanz,* is that in any set of data the mind sees a good form—one that is simple, continuous and bounded—and a com-prehensive form—one that takes account of a high proportion of the data (see section 24 above). The main law of information theory is that the information carried by one signal in a string of signals—say, a word in a sentence—is an inverse function of the probability of the signal occurring (see section 14 above). These laws have suggested to certain theorists that in aesthetic analysis they ought to be showing the effect on overall *gestalt* and information of every element in the work of art.

Moles is the best example of an information theory approach, Arnheim of a *gestalt* psychology one, Meyer of an approach involving both theories (see Bibliographical References). Meyer describes how the law of *prägnanz* dominates in our perception of music, giving us continuity, completion and closure: these expectations, by information theory, determine the information each element in the music will carry and also, in the way they are inhibited and fulfilled, its affective tone. Arnheim in similar fashion describes the operation of this law in our perception of visual art—particularly painting but also sculpture and architecture. He shows how the law operates in the production of different effects crucial to the eye: balance, light, movement, and so on. Finally, Moles looks in different works of art for the maximisation of information: the more information it has, the greater the work; the more information it can find in a work, the better an analysis.

The systematic analysis of non-literary works of art in *gestalt* terms promises, in whatever form it takes, to be of some interest and to avoid the drawbacks of technical and expressive analysis. It is worth mentioning one danger, however, which information theory brings with it. This is that the analyst may be led to take too intellectual a view of a work of art, he may have his attention directed only to effects of information or novelty. Information theory fails to answer two questions—why every work of art is so repetitive and why it is always worthwhile returning to a work of art. To the first question Moles says that repetition is necessary to get the message across, the human subject needing redundancy in the message (Moles 200). To the second, Meyer says that in the case of music repeated hearing remains interesting because one's experience between hearings will have shifted one's expectations and restored informative capacity to the music (Meyer 58). The replies are weak. The first makes art seem poorer than it might be, a sop to human weakness. The second is implausible: there may have been no musically significant experience between two equally enjoyable hearings of the same piece of music in the same performance.

Moles and Meyer are surely led astray when they put such stress on artistic information—the power of a work to challenge and surprise. What is of equal importance in music, architecture or painting is satisfaction. I mean the word etymologically : the repetition in a work, usually through variations, which ensures that the aesthetic subject is given 'enough', that he is satisfied and not just tantalised. It is a point of the most common experience that the human being enjoys having his expectations fulfilled —as rhyme fulfils expectations in poetry for instance. A work of art is satisfying only if this desire is indulged in some measure— the limit of the indulgence is precisely that at which the work ceases to be interesting or informative.

32. We have some idea now of what the extension of the linguistic model to the non-literary arts can mean. Just as in its extension to a literary art like narrative, the model fails to make theory possible but it does show the way to straight and systematic analysis. In the final sections of this chapter we must ask what it means to extend the model to the 'customary' arts.

The most obvious examples of 'customary' arts are fashion and cuisine, the arts discussed briefly in section 19. Other examples are to be found in the writings of social anthropologists and social psychologists (see Barthes 1964, Douglas 1973a and 1973b). The most interesting of them perhaps is the art of self-presentation, an art with which social psychologists have been particularly concerned of late (see Garfinkel, Goffman, Harré/ Secord). To present oneself in the sense in question is to see oneself as being or doing something—one can at least say what one is at, if asked—and to behave in such a way that this can also be seen by others. Thus, gestures like smiling and waving, and routines like welcoming a friend to one's house or bringing a conversation to an end, are examples of this art.

As in the case of the literary and non-literary arts there is a central argument for the extension of the linguistic model to customary arts : that is, for considering any piece of such art on the model of a sentence. The argument supposes an analogy between the sentence and the piece of art in question on two counts. The piece of art—an outfit, a menu or, let us say, a presentational procedure—is meaningful, since it expresses the mind of the person dressing up, eating out or presenting himself. And it is mechanical since it puts parts together under certain ordering constraints and with regard for certain contrasts : the parts in the outfit are the different garments, in the menu the dishes, in the presentational procedure the different expressions, facial and verbal, the bodily movements, the physical setting, and so on. What the argument asserts is that the piece of art produces its distinctive meaning precisely by the articulation of its parts.

There are two premises to the argument. The first is that the meaning of the whole depends on the meaning of its parts so that it changes if the meaning of any part changes. The second is that the meaning of a part is determined by its background contrasts with what might have replaced it without making nonsense of the whole. These premises hold good in the case of any piece of fashion, cuisine or presentation. They imply that any such piece of art produces its meaning by having its parts set up against appropriate contrasts. We must now consider, very briefly, what possibilities for studying customary arts are suggested by this conclusion.

33. The possibilities to consider are straight and systematic analysis, generative and descriptive theory. Straight analysis takes particular outfits, menus and presentational procedures and tries to account for their distinctive effects by particular patterns in their articulation. It may be pursued in a purely intuitive way or with the help of the commutation test mentioned in section 29. In the analysis of presentational procedures the commutation test has geen given the name 'garfinkelling', after Harold Garfinkel. To garfinkel is to vary an element in the procedure for a standard form of presentation and watch the effect on one's audience. Say I am travelling by bus and the conductor comes to give me my ticket. I perform every action according to the usual rite, glancing briefly up at the conductor's face and mumbling 'Five, please.' Every action, that is, but one : I offer the five-pence piece, not between my index finger and thumb, but on the back of my hand! The difference which this variation makes in my effect on the conductor will be the measure of the role played by the normal action in the normal presentation.

A second possible approach to the study of customary arts is systematic analysis. This is analysis pursued under the direction of an organised set of categories which claim to reflect important features of the art in question. The categories give the analyst terms in which to assess the significance of each element, by contrast with its possible replacements, in the piece of art. As with non-literary art the discovery of satisfactory categories of analysis is a problem with customary art. One of the reasons why the art of presentation has been so investigated of late may be that recently a set of categories has been proposed for its systematic analysis. The categories are generated by the metaphor of the stage. On the assumption that people are actors intent on producing and maintaining a particular definition of any situation, the analyst assesses every element in a presentational procedure for its significance from the point of view of role, setting, script, cue and so on (see Goffman, Harré/Secord).

The semiological analysis, straight or systematic, of pieces of customary art is clearly a respectable project. The only assumption it makes is that which the argument in section 32 yields: under our usual type of reading, it is that for any piece of customary art to be given meaning it must be assigned a structure which puts limits on what can replace any element in the piece. Neither form of analysis supposes that there is a 'language' of fashion, cuisine or presentation. Each depends on the linguistic model only for a useful formulation of its programme.

What about a generative or descriptive theory of customary art? Generative theory seems an unlikely prospect in every area though Harré and Secord make a faint suggestion that there is a generative grammar of presentational procedures to be uncovered (Harré/Secord 170). The same considerations apply here as in the literary and non-literary arts. With no piece of customary art is our intuitive sense of structure firm enough to bear representation in a grammar of strict recursive rules. We do indeed project a structure on any piece of art and it is this which accounts for the contrasts against which we see any element in the piece. The structure may be considered however as a *gestalt* for which we look in accordance with the general law of *prägnanz*, not as a form which we assign in conformity with strict rules.

Finally, what of descriptive theory? It is not a plausible project with the art of presentation but does look a possibility with fashion and cuisine. Probably, indeed, the best example of an attempt at descriptive semiological theory is that worked out by Barthes in his *Système de la Mode*. Barthes takes as his objects of study the captions which occur in *Elle* and *Jardin des Modes* in 1958–9, captions like *Un chandail à col fermé*, 'A sweater with fastened neck'. These captions define a 'string'—an incomplete outfit—and set down a basic structure for it : an object (the sweater), a variant (fastened) and a support of the variant (the neck). Barthes's theory consists in lists of things which can occur either as objects or supports, and lists of variants. These lists are divided into genera such that no two members of a genus of objects/supports can appear as object and support to one another and no two members of a genus of variants can be simultaneously variants on the same support : the genera represent clusters of items in distinctive paradigmatic contrast.

The criticism we have made in every case of descriptive theory is that, even where it is plausible, it is uninteresting. The criticism, unfortunately, is an obvious one in the present case also. All that Barthes's theory can do is show how many outfits are possible within the object-support-variant structure—physically possible, at that, not fashionably possible. It cannot offer an explanation of the differences in overall effect between one outfit and another because its characterisation of each is too abstract; what is distinctive about each outfit will not be reflected in the terms it uses. Its characterisation is abstract because this is required for the game of deducing the abstract possibilities of combination among the elements (see section 59 below).

This brings us to the end of our discussion of the range of the linguistic model. What the model makes possible in customary art, as in literary and non-literary art, is analysis of individual works, straight or systematic. It fails to produce theory because in none of these areas is there a 'language' to be found, whether in the sense of a generative grammar or a descriptive combinatory of elements. At this point it becomes necessary to speak in general of the role of models and to try to assess the value of the linguistic model in semiology. But, before taking up that task, we must discuss the development of the model for which Lévi-Strauss has been responsible.

BIBLIOGRAPHICAL REFERENCES TO II

R. Arnheim, *Art and Visual Perception*, London : Faber, 1956
H. S. Babb, ed., *Essays in Stylistic Analysis*, New York : Harvard Brace Jovanovich, 1972
S. Bann and J. E. Bowlt, ed., *Russian Formalism*, Edinburgh : Scottish Academic Press, 1973
R. Barthes, *Sur Racine*, Paris : Seuil, 1963
 Elements of Semiology (1964), London : Cape, 1967
 Critique et Vérité, Paris : Seuil, 1966a
 'Introduction a l'analyse structurale des recits', *Communications* 8, 1966b
 Système de la Mode, Paris : Seuil, 1967
 S/Z, Paris : Seuil, 1970
 'A Conversation' (1971) in Heath, McCabe and Prendergast (see below)
 Le Plaisir de Texte, Paris : Seuil, 1973
E. Benveniste, *Problèmes de Linguistique Générale*, Paris : Gallimard, 1966
R. Boudon, *The Uses of Structuralism*, London : Heinemann Educational, 1971
C. Bremond, *Logique du Recit*, Paris : Seuil, 1973
J. Culler, 'Structuralism', D.Phil. Dissertation, Oxford University, 1972
R. De George and F. De George, ed., *The Structuralists from Marx to Lévi-Strauss*, Garden City : Doubleday Anchor Books, 1972
G. Deleuze, *Différence et Répétition*, Paris : PUF, 2nd edition, 1972
J. Derrida, *La Voix et le Phénomène*, Paris : PUF, 1967a
 De la Grammatologie, Paris : Minuit, 1967b
 'Semiologie et Grammatologie' (1968) in J. Kristeva, et al., ed., *Essays in Semiotics*, The Hague : Mouton, 1971
G. Dorfles, 'Structuralism and Semiology in Architecture' in Jencks and Baird (see below)
M. Douglas, *Natural Symbols*, Harmondsworth : Penguin, 1973a
 ed., *Rules and Meanings*, Harmondsworth : Penguin, 1973b

O. Ducrot, et al., *Qu'est-ce que le Structuralisme?*, Paris : Seuil, 1968

M. Dufrenne, *Pour l'Homme*, Paris : Seuil, 1968

J. Ehrmann, ed., *Structuralism*, Garden City : Doubleday Anchor Books, 1970

U. Eco, 'Social Life as a Sign System' in Robey (see below)

V. Erlich, *Russian Formalism*, The Hague : Mouton, 1955

H. Garfinkel, *Studies in Ethnomethodology*, Englewood Cliffs, N.J. : Prentice-Hall, 1967

G. Genette, *Figures III*, Paris : Seuil, 1973

E. Goffman, *Asylums*, Harmondsworth : Penguin, 1968
  The Presentation of Self in Everyday Life, Harmondsworth : Penguin, 1969

A. J. Greimas, *Semantique Structurale*, Paris : Larousse, 1966
  Du Sens, Paris : Seuil, 1970

R. Harré, *Philosophies of Science*, Oxford University Press, 1972

R. Harré and P. F. Secord, *The Explanation of Social Behaviour*, Oxford : Blackwell, 1972

S. Heath, 'Ambiviolences', *Tel Quel*, 1972

S. Heath, C. McCabe and C. Prendergast, *Signs of the Times*, Cambridge : Granta, 1971

G. Hough, *Style and Stylistics*, London : Routledge and Kegan Paul, 1969

R. Jakobson and C. Lévi-Strauss, 'Charles Baudelaire's Les Chats' in Lane (see below)

C. Jencks and G. Baird, ed., *Meaning in Architecture*, London : Barrie and Jenkins, 1970

W. Kohler, *The Place of Value in a World of Facts*, New York : Liveright, 1938

J. Kristeva, *Le Texte du Roman*, The Hague : Mouton, 1970
  'The Semiotic Activity' (1971) in Heath, McCabe and Prendergast (see above)

M. Lane, *Structuralism: A Reader*, London : Cape, 1970

R. Mackay and E. Donato, ed., *The Language of Criticism and the Sciences of Man*, Baltimore : John Hopkins Press, 1970

C. Metz, *Essai sur la Signification au Cinema*, Paris : Klinsieck, Vol. 1, 1968; Vol. 2, 1972
  Langage et Cinema, Paris : Larousse, 1971

L. B. Meyer, *Emotion and Meaning in Music*, Chicago, 1956

A. Moles, *Information Theory and Aesthetic Perception*, Urbana : University of Illinois Press, 1966

C. Norberg-Schulz, *Intentions in Architecture*, London : Allan and Unwin, 1966

P. Pettit, 'Parmenides and Sartre', *Philosophical Studies* (Ireland) XVII (1968)

> *On the Idea of Phenomenology*, Dublin : Scepter, 1969
> 'A Theory of Justice?', *Theory and Decision IV*, 1974
> 'The Life-World and Role-Theory' in E. Pivcevic, ed., *Phenomenology and Philosophical Understanding*, Cambridge University Press, 1975

J. Piaget, *Structuralism*, London : Routledge and Kegan Paul, 1971

Poetics III, 1972

P. Portoghesi, *Rome of the Renaissance*, London : Phaidon, 1972

V. Propp, *Morphology of the Folktale*, Austin : University of Texas Press, 2nd ed., 1968

J. Rawls, *A Theory of Justice*, Oxford University Press, 1972

M. Riffaterre, 'Describing Poetic Structure' in Babb (see above)

D. Robey, ed., *Structuralism: An Introduction*, Oxford University Press, 1973

C. Rosen, *The Classical Style*, London : Faber, 1971

G. Ryle, 'Use and Usage', *Philosophical Review* LXII (1953)

F. Salzer, *Structural Hearing*, New York : Dover, 1962

J. P. Sartre, *Being and Nothingness*, London : Methuen, 1957

R. Scholes, *Structuralism in Literature*, London : Yale University Press, 1974

T. Sebeok, ed., *Style in Language*, Cambridge, Mass. : MIT Press, 1960

J. Summerson, *The Language of Architecture*, London : Methuen, 1966

Tel Quel, Theorie d'Ensemble, Paris : Seuil, 1968

T. Todorov, *Littérature et Signification*, Paris : Larousse, 1967

> 'Poétique' (1968) in O. Ducrot, et al. (see above)
> *Grammaire du Decameron*, The Hague : Mouton, 1969
> 'The Structural Analysis of Literature' (1973) in Robey (see above)

H. Wölfflin, *Classic Art*, London : Phaidon, 1968

III

A Development of the Model

34. In this chapter my concern is solely with Lévi-Strauss. It is surprising perhaps that I should consider his work as a development of the linguistic model rather than as an application of it : he is regarded after all as the father of structuralism. If structuralism is defined however as a programme for semiology then Lévi-Strauss's work must be considered as something more than simply structuralism. His interest is not primarily in revealing the mechanism by which meaning is produced in semiological objects. The point has been made by Mary Douglas. 'Lévi-Strauss is not content with revealing structure for its own sake. Structural analysis has long been a respectable tool of literary criticism and Lévi-Strauss is not interested in a mere literary exercise' (Douglas 57 : for other assessments see Boon, Gardner, Glucksman, Hayes/Hayes, Runciman, Simonis).

Lévi-Strauss's work resembles that of other French intellectuals who are sometimes regarded as structuralists too : Louis Althusser, the Marxian theorist, Michel Foucault, the historian of ideas, and Jacques Lacan, the Freudian psychoanalyst (see Bibliographical References). What these thinkers have in common is a rejection of phenomenology, particularly existentialism. Phenomenology would suggest a distinctive approach in anthropology and history of ideas, one that made of each a discipline of *Verstehen*, an attempt to project oneself through understanding and empathy into another age or culture (see, for example, Ricoeur 1960). Similarly phenomenology would suggest a distinctive reinterpretation of Freudian and Marxian analysis : each would become an investigation of external constraints, psychological and sociological, on the individual's capacity to give his own meaning to the world (see, for examples, Ricoeur 1950, 1965; Sartre 1943, 1960).

Althusser, Foucault, Lacan and Lévi-Strauss are 'anti-pheno-menologists' to a man : they all reject the standpoint of subjective consciousness taken by phenomenology. What a culture or an age, a personal unconscious or a social infrastructure does is not just provide conditions that make subjective consciousness possible. At least they do not do so in such a way that the conditions might be read off as part of the phenomenological description of consciousness—or even in such a way that if read off elsewhere, in scientific investigation, they might be easily integrated within the phenomenological description. According to the anti-phenomenologists, the conditions determine subjective consciousness to the extent that its self-understanding, the under-standing each man has of what he does and why he does it, is quite discontinuous with the understanding which a scientific study of those conditions yields : at the limit this study presents subjective consciousness as 'false consciousness', a consciousness sytematically beset by illusion about its own autonomy.

This is heady stuff and it is not surprising that each of the anti-phenomenologists looks for a concrete illustration of his thesis. They all find the required illustration in language. This is a system put into operation by the speaking subject which he may still fail to understand and which he may even misunder-stand—if he is a phenomenologist for instance who thinks that he gives words meaning by his own intentional disposition (see section 20 above). Language establishes a set of conditions on consciousness which each of the anti-phenomenologists compares with the set of conditions that he studies, particularly in respect of the unfamiliar character of language. Thus Althusser's 'ideology', Foucault's 'archive' (roughly, *Weltanschauung*), Lacan's 'unconscious' and Lévi-Strauss's 'mythology' all become 'languages' in their own right.

This, however, does not make structuralists of the anti-pheno-menologists, at least by the definition operated here; indeed, Althusser and Foucault explicitly disavow structuralism (Althusser 1968, 7; Foucault 1969, 15). Althusser, Foucault and Lacan cannot be counted as structuralists for a strong reason : there is nothing in ideology, the archive or the unconscious to correspond properly to the sentence in language. This crucial disanalogy means that the linguistic model cannot be pressed in these areas, even in a purely analytic way. Lévi-Strauss cannot be counted as

a structuralist for a weaker reason : his scientific ambitions go
well beyond structuralism.

35.   Lévi-Strauss's work falls into three divisions : his analysis
of kinship systems (Lévi-Strauss—henceforth LS—1949), his
discussion of systems of classification (LS 1962a and b) and his
analysis of myth (LS 1958a and b, 1964, 1966, 1968, 1971a and
b). By his own account the second part of his work is not of
intrinsic importance, it is commentary rather than analysis. He
attaches importance only to his analysis of kinship and his
analysis of myth.

For the same reason that I do not discuss Althusser, Foucault
or Lacan, I shall not discuss Lévi-Strauss's analysis of kinship.
It is not a semiological analysis because there is nothing in kinship to correspond properly to the sentence in language. What
holds in common between language and kinship systems is something very abstract—suggestive perhaps but not semiological.
Lévi-Strauss claims to achieve his analysis of kinship 'by treating
marriage regulations and kinship systems as a kind of language,
a set of processes permitting the establishment, between individuals and groups, of a certain kind of communication. That the
mediating factor, in this case, should be the *women of the group*,
who are circulated, between clans, lineages, or families, in place
of the *words of the group*, which are circulated between individuals, does not at all change the fact that the essential aspect of
the phenomenon is identical in both cases' (LS 1958b, 61).

The 'language' of kinship in the sense required by the analogy
is the set of possible kinship arrangements, the 'sentence', if it
can be called that, the arrangement of a particular community.
This arrangement is not a proper analogue to the sentence
because it is not something the construction of which requires
knowledge of the language. In order to choose an outfit for
myself I must know the language of fashion, in the loose sense
that I can foresee the effect of changing this or that element in
the outfit. In order for a community to construct a kinship
arrangement no comparable knowledge is required. Thus we do
not feel that the occurrence of the arrangement is to be explained
in terms of a significant choice, however unconscious, but rather
as an historical accident. The only one aware of the 'language'
of kinship and able to see the arrangement of a community in

significant contrast with other arrangements is the man who is informed about various communities and knows about the operation of different arrangements: typically, the professional anthropologist. He is the only one who is master of the language of kinship and it would be arbitrary of him to credit the communities he studies with a similar mastery. Thus the study of kinship systems is not the examination of an activity corresponding to speech, an ability comparable to linguistic competence. The only aspect of the study which is semiological is the analysis of kinship terminology on the lines of the structural semantics mentioned in section 8, but this aspect is not basic in Lévi-Strauss's scheme (see Scheffler-Lounsbury—listed in I).

36. In the analysis of myth Lévi-Strauss's interest does sometimes seem to be an orthodox semiological one: for instance when he reaffirms, in the last volume of *Mythologiques*, that the intention of the structuralist is 'to discover why works captivate us' (LS 1971a, 573). These works include the product of the individual author and that product when it is absorbed by a collective tradition in such a way that it becomes a myth: 'structural analysis can apply legitimately to myths produced by the collective tradition and to works of a single author since the programme will be the same here and there' (LS 1971a, 560). An orthodox semiological approach would take this structural analysis in one of the senses allowed by the tree of options described in section 27—most likely, in the sense of straight or systematic analysis. The aim would be to explain how the works produce those effects of meaning crucial to their understanding and appreciation.

This is not Lévi-Strauss's aim because he is not interested in orthodox analysis. There are two obstacles to such analysis in the study of myth and it is perhaps these which put him off. The first is that there are always numerous versions of any single myth; this, because myth belongs essentially to a collective, oral tradition. 'Mythical thought is by its nature transformative. Once it is born each myth changes with the change of narrator, whether this be within the tribal group or in being passed on from people to people. Certain elements fall away, others replace them, sequences are inverted: the distorted structure passes through a series of states of which the successive changes still maintain the character of a group' (LS 1971a 603-4). An orthodox approach is capable of analysing how meaning effects are produced in a single text. It is not clear what it should do when there are an indefinite number of versions of the 'same' myth, none of them the canonical text.

The second obstacle to the orthodox analysis of myth is more serious. It is that the meaning of a myth or version of a myth is not given to the alien anthropologist in such a way that he can correlate structural devices in the myth with effects of meaning. He cannot operate the commutation test for example. More generally, he cannot control the account of structural devices in the myth by the principle of reflective equilibrium. He lacks the native intuition against which to measure semiological analysis.

Can the anthropologist not enter the native's world through empathy and understanding and learn the required intuition? For Lévi-Strauss, no—because of his anti-phenomenology. He regards the project of *Verstehen* as intrinsically fallible, one that cannot mark off insight from illusion. 'Because we are prisoners of subjectivity we cannot understand things simultaneously from within and without; and we cannot understand them from within unless we are born within, unless we are effectively within' (LS 1963, 637; see also 643-4 and LS 1960, 16). What Lévi-Strauss suggests, paradoxically, is that any intuition into the meaning of myth, any understanding of the world of that myth, is only possible after analysis and explanation. 'Since we_study "human sciences", since we are men who study men, we are able to give ourselves the luxury of putting ourselves in their place. But that is the last moment, it is the final pleasure, which we allow ourselves when we put the question : Is that plausible? Does it work if I try it on myself? Thus the retrieval of meaning seems to me, from the point of view of method, to be secondary and derived' (LS 1963, 640; see also 1962a, 176 and—for a broader assessment of *Verstehen*—LS 1962b, 250).

37. Lévi-Strauss avoids the obstacles to an orthodox semiological analysis of myth by giving himself a project which makes such analysis seem pedestrian. The structural analysis of myth which he seeks turns out to be something much more radical than might be expected. This appears when he says that its justification 'lies in the unique and most economical coding system to

which it can reduce messages of a most disheartening complexity, and which previously appeared to defeat all attempts to decipher them' (LS 1964, 147). What he wants in the study of myth is not a replication of what literary critics offer in the study of narrative but a science of immense theoretical power. 'What I am concerned to clarify is not so much what there is *in* myths . . . as the system of axioms and postulates defining the best possible code, capable of conferring a common significance on unconscious formulations which are the work of minds, societies, and civilisations chosen from among those most remote from one another' (LS 1964, 12).

His stated ambitions enable Lévi-Strauss to put aside the obstacles mentioned in the last section. The objective of his analysis is a structure which he takes to remain constant from version to version of a myth; thus the first difficulty is dissolved by postulate. 'Because it [the myth, once it is produced] will be immediately released to an oral tradition, as that develops among peoples without writing, only the levels of structure which rest on common foundations will remain stable; the probabilistic levels will display an extreme variability, something which is a function of the personality of successive narrators' (LS 1971a, 560).

Meaning, surface meaning, is a requirement in any myth; without it a myth would have no interest (see LS 1971a, 573). The object of Lévi-Strauss's concern, however, the constant from version to version of a myth, is something deeper than meaning, something to which meaning can be reduced. Thus the second difficulty disappears too. 'Within my perspective meaning is never a basic phenomenon, it is always reducible. In other words, behind every sense there is a non-sense and not vice-versa. For me meaning is always phenomenal' (LS 1963, 637).

Despite his revision of the structuralist enterprise Lévi-Strauss still wants to show why myths captivate their audience. This means that he has to explain how the sort of structure which he wants to find in myths can engage the human mind. The challenge leads us towards his philosophy of man but to prepare ourselves for discussing it we must look at the linguistic model on which he formulates his enterprise.

38. In his earliest articles Lévi-Strauss takes his lead from

linguistics. 'For centuries the humanities and the social sciences have resigned themselves to contemplating the world of the natural and exact sciences as a kind of paradise which they will never enter. And all of a sudden there is a small door which is being opened between the two fields, and it is linguistics which has done it' (LS 1958a, 70). The linguistics which he introduced as guide for his own work and that which has continued to dominate structuralism in anthropology is Jakobson's phonology. 'It is important that you should appreciate that, in so far as structuralist social anthropology depends upon a borrowing of ideas from the linguists, these ideas come mainly from the theory of comparative *phonology* rather than from the general theory of *transformational grammar.* That may be a pity, yet it is so' (Leach 1973, 40). Thus Edmund Leach in a recent lecture.

Not only does Lévi-Strauss take his lead from phonology however, he also tends to reduce the whole of linguistics to the discipline. 'Linguistics teaches us precisely that structural analysis cannot be applied to words directly, but only to words previously broken down into phonemes. *There are no necessary relationships at the vocabulary level*' (LS 1958a, 36). It seems that he overestimates the significance of structural phonology : 'this phonological revolution . . . consists in the discovery that meaning results always from the combination of elements which are not themselves meaningful' (LS 1963, 637). 'Results from' is ambiguous. It might mean 'presupposes', something quite uncontroversial. What it tends to mean in Lévi-Strauss is nearer to 'is produced by'.

Phonology gives Lévi-Strauss the idea that the only way to look at language or any similar system is as a set of units which can be defined in specific terms and then examined for their syntagmatic constraints and paradigmatic contrasts; he thinks only in terms of the first of the two approaches distinguished in section 7, i.e. the paradigmatic one (see, for example, LS 1971a, 611–14). This dependence on phonology however gives Lévi-Strauss's work more than its general methodological direction. It has two specific effects on the content of that work which it is essential that we understand.

In the development of structural phonology, particularly with Jakobson and Halle, three tendencies have been evident : the search for a small set of universal distinctive features, by which to define the phonemes of all languages, the description of those features in acoustic rather than articulatory terms and the insistence on staying with the binary or two-valued distinctive feature (see Lyons 1969, 127—cited above in I). The first and last of these tendencies—universalism and binarism—are reflected directly in Lévi-Strauss's anthropology.

His binarism is presented as a general theory about the way the human mind works. Not only the thought process but also perceptual experience displays binary organisation. 'The prime matter, if one may use that term, of immediate visual perception consists already of such binary oppositions as those of the simple and the complex, the light and the dark, the light on a dark background and the dark on a light background, the movement from above downwards and from below upwards, at a right angle and at an oblique one, etc.' (LS 1971a, 619). Lévi-Strauss appeals to psychological research in defence of his claim but it is clear that he gives the claim philosophical status. Thus he argues—though without giving detail—that consciousness of the self presupposes, not so much consciousness of the opposition between the self and the other, as consciousness of the other as being already contained within different oppositions (see LS 1971a, 539–40). He means presumably that I can be conscious of the other—and therefore conscious of the self which I oppose to it—only if I can give the other 'op-positional' identity of its own. He assumes that the oppositions which operate in such a case take the simplest binary form.

The second specific effect of phonology on Lévi-Strauss is to make him universalist in his approach. It leads him to assume that the binary oppositions on which any semiological system is constructed are not particular to that system but belong to a class of universal oppositions. They are like the oppositions which recur in phonemic systems and define distinctive features—for example the opposition between voiced and unvoiced. His universalism appears in his readiness to move away from the particular object of analysis—the particular myth or version of a myth—to compare it in increasingly general terms with other objects; this we shall see later in the chapter. Where others are more impressed by diversity and contrast he finds an 'astounding similarity between myths collected in widely different regions' (LS 1958a, 208). The motto which defines his attitude and guides his analysis is one that he attributes explicitly to Jakobson and Halle : 'The supposed multiplicity of features proves to be largely illusory' (LS 1958a, 83).

39.   The dominance of the phonological model in his thinking leads Lévi-Strauss into a reductionism in his philosophy of man. The reductionism takes two forms, vertical and horizontal (see Pettit 1972, 54–7). The vertical form consists in the assertion of the primacy of the unconscious over the conscious. Saussure had asserted that the linguistic system works unconsciously—'the very ones who use it daily are ignorant of it' (Saussure 73—cited above in I)—and this was reaffirmed by the phonologists (see LS 1958a, 33). The emphasis is reflected in Lévi-Strauss who sees in phonology investigations 'which have reached beyond the superficial conscious and historical phenomena to attain fundamental and objective realities consisting of systems of relations which are the products of unconscious thought processes' (LS 1958a, 58). His structuralism only began to develop as he raised the possibility that all forms of social life 'consist of systems of behaviour that represent the projection, on the level of conscious and socialised thought, of universal laws which regulate the unconscious activities of the mind' (LS 1958a, 59).

The horizontal form of reductionism in Lévi-Strauss receives even more emphasis. It complements the vertical form, consisting in the idea that at their unconscious level, as formal systems of oppositions, the semiological forms of life in any one society must be expected to be closely related—and indeed that there may be some relation to be found too between the systems operative in different societies. The possibility of reducing the horizontal variety of semiological forms to a formula defining their relationship arises for Lévi-Strauss once he allows each form to be taken as a system of binary oppositions described in universal terms; such a system can be compared and correlated with other systems. 'Once we have defined these differential structures, there is nothing absurd about inquiring whether they belong strictly to the sphere considered or whether they may be encountered (often in transformed fashion) in other spheres of the same society or in different societies' (LS 1958a, 87). Indeed, not only is there nothing absurd about the inquiry : it is based on a reasonable expectation. 'If there were no relations at all, that would lead us to assume that the human mind is a kind of jumble—that there is no connection at all between what the mind is doing on one level and what the mind is doing on another level' (LS 1958a, 79).

40. Lévi-Strauss's reductionist philosophy puts the case for a determinism of a structuralist variety. He believes that the human mind—the *esprit humain* which has puzzled his kindest critics (see Leach 1969, 25–7)—is determined in its expressions by the unconscious laws of the semiological systems it puts into operation. He means, apparently, not just that these laws describe conditions under which the mind works but that the work of the mind is the direct product of those laws : again 'presupposes' slips into 'is produced by'. 'Starting from ethnographic experience, I have always aimed at drawing up an inventory of mental patterns, to reduce apparently arbitrary data to some kind of order, and to attain a level at which a kind of necessity becomes apparent, underlying the illusions of liberty' (LS 1964, 10).

The conception of the human subject against which he pits his own view is naturally the phenomenological one. The phenomenological subject, author of meaning and value in its own world, is for Lévi-Strauss an 'intolerable spoiled child who for too long has held the philosophical scene and prevented any serious work, drawing exclusive attention to itself' (see LS 1971a, 614–15).

Metaphysically, Lévi-Strauss opposes phenomenology with a blunt materialism. The mind, so his analysis reveals, is a 'thing among things' (LS 1964, 10; see also 27). Methodologically, he opposes it with an approach that refuses to be charmed by what is revealed of the mind in consciousness. 'Like the physical sciences the human sciences must realise that the reality of their object of study is not entirely confined to the level at which the subject perceives it ... It is the right of the political thinker, the moralist and the philosopher to occupy the stage which they consider the only honourable one and to barricade themselves there. But they must not claim the right to keep everyone else with them and to prohibit others who want to investigate quite different problems from adjusting the control of the microscope, changing the focus, and thus presenting a different object behind the one to which they love to give exclusive contemplation' (LS 1971a, 570–1).

Two historical parallels serve to illustrate nicely the philosophy of man adopted by Lévi-Strauss. The first he draws himself, with Marx and Freud. He associates geology with the disciplines set up by these thinkers and in the three claims to find the 'three mistresses' of his thought. 'All three show that understanding consists in reducing one type of reality to another, that the true reality is never the most manifest, and that the nature of truth is already evident in the care which it takes to conceal itself' (LS 1955, 44).

The second historical parallel was drawn by Paul Ricoeur but is accepted by Lévi-Strauss (see LS 1963, 633; 1964, 11). It is a parallel with Kant who also makes of the mind a principle of categorisation which works unconsciously. In Kant however this principle is ultimately a personal one, the transcendental subject in which the unity of the self is rooted. Lévi-Strauss's philosophy, in Ricoeur's words, is a Kantianism without a transcendental subject. Here the principle of categorisation, as Lévi-Strauss himself admits, 'takes on the character of an autonomous object, independent of any subject' (LS 1964, 11). It is something to be revealed therefore not in any phenomenological description, nor in the sort of philosophical deduction favoured by Kant, but in the structural analysis of its products, among them myths.

41.   We need a clearer notion of Lévi-Strauss's philosophy of man than that offered by an understanding of its linguistic origins (sections 38 and 39) or its historical parallels (section 40). We may find it in the illustration of that philosophy represented by his account of music. Music works through two 'grids' he claims : the natural grid of physiological rhythm and the cultural grid of the musical scale—i.e., the tonic sol-fa. These grids determine the disposition of a listener and a particular musical composition engages him because of the disposition. 'The musical emotion springs precisely from the fact that at each moment the composer withholds or adds more or less than the listener anticipates on the basis of a pattern that he thinks he can guess, but that he is incapable of wholly divining, because of his subjection to a dual periodicity: that of his respiratory system, which is determined by his individual nature, and that of the scale, which is determined by his training. If the composer withholds more than we anticipate, we experience a delicious falling sensa-

tion; we feel we have been torn from a stable point on the musical ladder and thrust into the void, but only because the support that is waiting for us was not in the expected place. When the composer withholds less, the opposite occurs : he forces us to perform gymnastic exercises more skilful than our own' (LS 1964, 17).

What his determinism leads Lévi-Strauss to say in the case of music is that both grids, the natural and the cultural, are necessary. He takes up the case of serial music where, with an 'unweighted' scale of notes all separated by half-tones, no cultural grid is presupposed or even allowed. Here he thinks that we have an attempt to remove music from the determining effect of a common cultural grid shared by listeners. 'Serial music sets itself up as a conscious product of the mind and an assertion of its liberty' (LS 1964, 27). This, it appears, is precisely the sort of assertion that his philosophy would put down as vain and illusory. He holds out little hope of success for serial music—and that little, only ironically : 'It may therefore turn out that serial music belongs to a universe in which the listener could not be carried along by its impetus but would be left behind. In vain would he try to catch up; with every passing day it would appear more distant and unattainable. Soon it would be too far away to affect his feelings; only the idea of it would remain accessible, before eventually fading away into the dark vault of silence, where men would recognise it only in the form of brief and fugitive scintillations' (LS 1964, 26).

It cannot be quite true however that Lévi-Strauss regards serial music as entirely vain, a musical expression of the phenomenological illusion of liberty. The development which it would represent of music—by his own characterisation of it—is precisely the development which the novel represents of myth—again by his own characterisation of the novel. 'It is as if music and literature had divided the heritage of myth. In becoming modern with Frascobaldi and Bach music acquired its form while the novel, born about the same time, took over "deformalised" remnants of myth and, freed from then on of the constraints of symmetry, found the means of constituting a free narrative' (LS 1971a, 583). Here it seems that Lévi-Strauss's reductionism and determinism do not extend to all the works of man, that above—or perhaps below—a certain limit, man is free.

What may save his philosophy in his own mind is that he does not have much time for the products of freedom. Certainly he does not have high regard for serial music. And even his view of the free narrative is not very flattering. Consider the account which he gives of a myth which transforms itself into such a narrative. 'In following the same myth from south to north one notices first an attenuation : this affects on the one hand the length and richness of the narrative and on the other the dramatic intensity of motifs, as if the intrigue had collapsed and contracted at the same time' (LS 1971b, 133). If the 'savage' mind—the mind in myth or in music—is less 'free' than the 'civilised'—and Lévi-Strauss never says so unequivocally—this does not mean that it is inferior (see LS 1966, 473–5).

42.   The question which led us in section 37 to ask about Lévi-Strauss's philosophy of man was, how does the sort of structure which he claims to find in myths engage the human mind. Why it engages the mind is reasonably clear—at least it is clear what Lévi-Strauss would say : the mind is essentially a structuring agent and there is really no question to be answered. But how does the structure in myth make its impact on the mind? Lévi-Strauss's answer is to draw a parallel between myth and music. This parallel is a natural one after our discussion of his philosophy of man; it generates his theory of myth, an empirical theory which fits in nicely with that philosophy.

A myth, like any other story, is a construction in language, a literary narrative. It might appear therefore that it is to be understood in a sequential reading of the sentences that embody it, that understanding it means following the narrative. Lévi-Strauss does not think so. Myth may be language but it is language with a difference : the significance of the myth is not the surface meaning produced by the language. 'Myth is language functioning on an especially high level where meaning succeeds practically at "taking off" from the linguistic ground on which it keeps rolling' (LS 1958a, 210).

The significance of a myth lies in a structure which it brings into play, subtly, in the story it tells : the structure may not be explicitly recognised by the native but it will be appreciated. The structure consists in the polarisation of certain realities familiar to the native and important to him. The myth plays with this polarisation and produces the impression of resolving it, an impression which is extremely satisfying for the native. This function served by myth is exactly the sort of function which music serves. 'Music fulfils a role comparable to that of myth. A myth coded in sounds rather than words, the musical work provides an interpretative grid, a matrix of relations which filters and organises lived experience, substitutes itself for lived experience and produces the blessed illusion that contradictions can be overcome and difficulties resolved' (LS 1971a, 589–90).

Lévi-Strauss's idea seems to be that the significance of a piece of music does not lie in the sequence of sounds which it represents but in the structure of sounds, the contrasting intervals, tonalities, phrases and so on, that it presupposes and puts into play. Similarly the significance of a myth lies in the structure, the contrasting themes, which it puts into play. It is not just that the myth could have no dramatic value without that structure already existing it in the native's mind and world. The whole value of the myth seems to be that it presents that structure to the native and allows him, albeit unconsciously, to come to terms with it—even gives him the feeling that the polarisation of the structure can be overcome, that it is not something absolute.

Spelt out, the analogy with music gives Lévi-Strauss two propositions about myth : these are two sides to his theory. The first is that myth is non-linear or non-sequential—the time of myth, as he likes to say, is reversible (see LS 1958a, 209–12). What he means is that a myth is essentially repetitive, returning again and again to the same points instead of just getting on with the story. The nature of myth is to resist linear reading, to suspend non-reversible time. It does this because its task is to exhibit a timeless structure, impressing it on the minds of the audience by repetition of the elements of the structure.

The second proposition about myth which Lévi-Strauss derives from the musical analogy bears on the nature of the structure which myth presents non-linearly, the polarised character which makes the structure interesting for the native and worth presenting. He puts the proposition in rather formal language. 'The purpose of myth is to provide a logical model capable of overcoming a contradiction (an impossible achievement if, as it happens, the contradiction is real)' (LS 1958a, 229). This statement suggests that the polarisation has a strict logical form and a definite social status—that it is a contradiction felt in the society at large. Neither suggestion is borne out in Lévi-Strauss's analyses and is scarcely worth examining. Mary Douglas offers a useful word of policy here when she says : 'I do not think it is fair to such an ebullient writer to take him literally' (Douglas, 50).

A final comment worth making about Lévi-Strauss's use of the musical analogy to generate a theory of myth is that he pre-supposes something like the motivic analysis of music mentioned in section 31. Music is non-linear not just in the sense of being generally repetitive; it is, specifically, the repetition of a single motif. That motif takes the form of an opposition which the piece of music tries to overcome at different levels. He has this to say about Ravel's 'Bolero'. 'The melody by tonal oscillations, the rhythm by its internal duality, are poised between symmetry and asymmetry; this appears on the one hand in the hesitation between binary and ternary, on the other in the hesitation between a serene tonality and an anxious one' (LS 1971a, 594). This reading of the 'Bolero' allows Lévi-Strauss to look at the work as an attempt to 'reconcile these contraries'; thus the significance of the work becomes a deep-lying motivic one. Here we can see the kind of musical theory which motivates his theory of myth.

43.   We have seen how Lévi-Strauss, confronted with difficulties raised by myth, deserts 'surface' analysis in favour of 'depth' analysis of meaning and how he justifies this analysis in his philosophy of man and, more particularly, in the theory of myth into which that philosophy leads him. It is time now to consider the precise method of analysis which he develops in his study of myth. Later I shall go on to criticise the method and, by implication, the philosophy and the theory that underlie it.

Lévi-Strauss's first statement of method is in a 1955 paper on 'The Structural Study of Myth' (see LS 1958a). He says that to be analysed a myth must be broken down first of all into units. These would correspond on our original model to the words in a sentence; they are something like the 'functions' into which Propp dissolves Russian folk tales. He decides on summarising the myth in snappy sentences and putting the sentences on index cards : the cards represent the units of the myth. So far we are in line with standard semiological analysis. However Lévi-Strauss now argues that since myth is non-linear, since it is repetitive, this distinctive aspect should be reflected in our summary. We must be able to see in our sequence of cards that the 'same' units are recurring at intervals, that the pattern of the cards is something like 1, 2, 4, 7, 8, 2, 3, 4, 6, 8, etc. If we can get our cards into this shape a further step is then possible. We can put the 1's, 2's, 3's and so on together in columns, forming a matrix of such a kind that the rows represent different sequences in the myth. This matrix is a perspicuous way of representing the myth because it allows us to see its linear and non-linear structure simultaneously. Each unit will normally link an event with a subject, it will be a relation, so each column will be a bundle of relations. What we want to discover in particular is how those bundles of relations are played off against one another in the myth.

In his 1955 paper Lévi-Strauss gives a sample analysis of the Theban 'version' of the Oedipus myth, in some of its 'variant' sequences. After sorting his cards he produces the accompanying

Cadmos seeks his
sister Europa, rav-
ished by Zeus

                                        Cadmos kills
                                        the dragon

            The Spartoi kill
            one another

                                                    Labdacos (Laios's
                                                      father)=*lame*(?)
                    Oedipus kills his
                    father, Laios   Laios (Oedipus's
                                                    father)=*left-
                                                    sided*(?)

                                        Oedipus kills
                                        the sphinx

                                                      Oedipus=*swollen-
                                                      foot*(?)

Oedipus marries his
mother, Jocasta

                          Eteocles kills his
                          brother, Polynices

Antigone buries her
brother, Polynices,
despite prohibition

matrix to represent the myth; in it each column is a bundle of significant relations, each row a sequence in the myth or—look at the fourth column—a significant suggestion.

Lévi-Strauss's procedure is to look at the pattern among the columns—as distinct from looking at the linear sequence given in reading row by row. The first column, he says, features the overrating of blood relations, the second the underrating of them. The third column represents a denial of the autochthonous origin of man since it shows a man killing a monster born of earth in order that his kind may live. The fourth column represents the persistence of man's autochthonous origin since it is a universal theme in mythology that men born of the earth cannot at first walk properly.

This characterisation of the matrix enables Lévi-Strauss to define the deep significance of the myth. What we have, he says, is a curious logical formulation of the problem of reconciling two conflicting views of man's origin : the theory that he is born of the earth and the knowledge that he is born of man and woman. The myth resolves the conflict—only notionally of course—by equating the blood relationship and the earth relationship. The two are equivalent—the logic really is curious—because each involves a 'contradiction' : in the one case that between columns 1 and 2, in the other that between columns 3 and 4. 'By a correlation of this type, the overrating of blood relations is to the underrating of blood relations as the attempts to escape autochthony is to the impossibility to succeed' (LS 1958a, 216).

44.   The details of the analysis are of little interest. In general it is clear that it bears out Lévi-Strauss's philosophy of man and, more specifically, his theory of myth. The myth is presented as a narrative which interests its hearers not because of its linear pattern—the story which it tells, to greater or lesser dramatic effect—but because of the deep-lying polarisation, the structure of oppositions, which it presents to them and pretends to resolve.

What is even more striking about the analysis is that it reflects in detail Lévi-Strauss's chosen linguistic model and, in part because it does this, meets the obstacles facing an orthodox analysis. It reflects the linguistic model because it is both binarist and universalist in tendency. The myth is shown to be built on binary oppositions—between columns 1 and 2 and between columns 3 and 4—and indeed to present in binary form the conflict which it claims to resolve between the two theories of man's origin. The analysis is universalist in the sense that the terms involved in the basic oppositions are described in a universally understandable language. Everywhere there are 'blood relations', everywhere it is possible to think of man as 'autochthonous' or 'born of the earth' : the descriptions are not culturally specific. Thus Lévi-Strauss can appeal to Pueblo mythology in asserting that autochthonous men are often taken to be incapable of walking properly.

Because it is universalist, Lévi-Strauss's analysis meets the difficulty that, not being native to the mythic world, the analyst cannot be sure of understanding in specific cultural terms the surface meaning of the myth, its linear content. What he has to understand, it now appears, is something that can be described in general terms, terms universal to cultures. All that is presupposed in the analyst is a knowledge of what it means to be born of man and woman, what it might mean to be born of earth. It is true that at the end of his analysis Lévi-Strauss talks of how the myth had a sharp point in a culture where mankind was taken to be autochthonous but this can be taken as exercise of that understanding and empathy which he allows to follow analysis : 'meaning is not directly perceived but deduced, reconstructed from an analysis of syntax' (LS 1963, 639).

The second difficulty which his analysis meets is that of there being many versions of any one myth. In the case considered the variant sequences might be regarded as versions, and in this sense the analysis allows all known versions and, if it is a correct analysis, any others that come to light to be placed within the analytic pattern. Thus one analysis serves for all versions though it can be worked out on the basis of a few. The same is true when we consider versions in the more proper sense in which the matrix given represents just one version, the Theban one. What Lévi-Strauss suggests is that other versions should be broken down in similar two-dimensional charts and the charts ranged behind one another to form a three-dimensional order. Thus we could examine not just the pattern among the columns of any one version but the pattern among the groups formed by the corresponding columns of all the versions : the examination should reveal the recurrence of the original pattern, 'the structural law of the myth' (LS 1958a, 217). Here again one analysis serves for all versions though it can be worked out without considering all. The myth analysed consists, equally, in all its versions. 'Our method thus eliminates a problem which has, so far, been one of the main obstacles to the progress of mythological studies, namely, the quest for the *true* version, or the *earlier* one' (LS 1958a, 216).

It is worth noting that within any version—in the proper sense —of a myth there is another type of repetition or 'slating' possible besides the repetition of sequences which, column-wise, have the same significance, the same structural role. This appears in Lévi-Strauss's analysis of 'The Story of Asdiwal', a Tsimshian myth from the Pacific coast of Canada. In a single version of the myth he reveals different 'schemes' in operation, 'various levels on which the myth evolves: geographic, economic, sociological, and cosmological' (LS 1958b, 1). The function of this repetition is the same as that of the repetition of sequences: 'to render the structure of the myth apparent' (LS 1958a, 227). Where the sequences replicate different elements in the basic structure of the myth, the schemes carry that structure at different levels: thus thy serve to 'transmit the same message' (LS 1958b, 14).

45. A question worth raising here, in parentheses, is whether Lévi-Strauss's approach looks for a correlate to 'language' in the analysis of myth. Does it look beyond the analysis of particular myths—if you like, particular versions of a myth—to the reconstruction, in the form of a theory, of the 'language' presupposed by those myths? The answer is that it does but that the theory sought looks in no way like the generative and descriptive theories mentioned in chapter II.

What the theory claims to reveal in a particular range of myths is the key structure or opposition put into play, under distinct transformations, in those myths. The structure is the message which the different myths 'encode'. But what is the 'language' of the myths? The answer nearest to Lévi-Strauss's thinking is: the set of possible encodings (see LS 1971a, 566).

This set of encodings is presumed by Lévi-Strauss to be exhausted for a given message in any given range of myths. Myths shift in form with change of narrator and change of social circumstances; thus they come to offer different encodings of the original message (see LS 1971a, 560, 603–4; also 1964, 332). He assumes that over a certain period they are bound to run through the full set of possible encodings. 'It is very rare for a mythological system, if it is at all resourceful, not eventually to exhaust all the possible codings of a single message' (LS 1964, 332).

This assumption is tied to a second one which sets up the idea of a 'language' of myth. This second assumption is that the set of possible encodings is limited and ordered. It is not a more or less open set of particular items but a closed set of abstractly definable possibilities: the possibilities are defined in terms of the possible transformations. This idea of the 'language' of myth is already evident in Lévi-Strauss's 1955 essay on the structural analysis of myth. 'By systematically using this kind of analysis it becomes possible to organise all the known variants of a myth into a set forming a kind of permutation group, the two variants placed at the far ends being in a symmetrical, though inverted, relationship to each other' (LS 1958a, 223).

46.   Before discussing his use of it in *Mythologiques* I propose to offer a critique of Lévi-Strauss's method of myth analysis. The method, to offer a rough account of it, is hypothetico-deductive rather than inductive; this, in line with most scientific procedures (see LS 1958a, 211). No amount of mere observation can reveal the sort of structure that Lévi-Strauss finds in the Oedipus myth or the story of Asdiwal. It is only in the light of a preconceived hypothesis that such structure can become visible. The hypothesis may be formed in the course of the analysis—it is then grounds for revision as well as prediction—but at crucial points it will be needed to motivate the required description of various aspects of the myth. Without Lévi-Strauss's hypothesis who would think of taking 'Antigone buries her brother' as an overrating of blood relations or 'The Spartoi kill one another' as an underrating.

What form does the hypothesis take? Apparently it must be a hypothesis about the 'structural law' of the myth, the basic opposition at work there. Only a strong hypothesis of this type is sufficient to give the abstract terms required for describing the units of the myth and putting them in columns. Again think of how unlikely it is that one would describe and order the units on the plan given in section 43 if one did not have an idea of the structural law one was going to find at work in the myth.

Where does Lévi-Strauss get his hypothesis? What gives him

D

his key idea in the analysis of Oedipus? Certainly not the free play of imagination since there is no reason why imagination should light on precisely this idea, this hypothesis. The theory of myth which he works out under the influence of his philosophy is clearly the source of inspiration. It suggests to him that in each myth he should find a binary opposition at play which is not specific to one version of the myth. Find it, he does.

Nothing in these comments is a criticism of Lévi-Strauss. There are good grounds for arguing that the hypothetico-deductive procedure is standard in science (see Popper), that it is often conducted under the dominance of a theory accepted on other grounds (see Harré—cited below in IV), and even that it is subject to the influence of various cultural pressures (see Kuhn, Young). Lévi-Strauss's procedure does not show up badly on the present scene in philosophy of science. His analysis may be a response to the difficulties facing orthodox analysis and at the same time the expression of an unbalanced understanding of linguistic analysis. His theory of myth may not be just a working hypothesis but something accepted—in part at least—on philosophical grounds and on the grounds of a satisfying analogy. His analysis may bring a rich idea to sparse data and use it to govern the description of the data. None of this however is exceptional. What he pursues may yet be science (see Mepham, Nutini).

The objection to Lévi-Strauss's method is a down-to-earth one. It is that the sort of hypothesis that he puts up in the analysis of Oedipus or any other myth is just not falsifiable. I leave as an open question the extent to which one hypothesis may be criticised in terms of another: this is under debate in contemporary philosophy of science (see Feyerabend). All I suppose is that a hypothesis must be such that when it is faced with the data it is possible that no fit may be found. This is to say that in a weak sense at least the hypothesis must be falsifiable.

47. Lévi-Strauss's transformational hypothesis—the name will be convenient for reference—is not falsifiable for many reasons. First of all, the formation of the hypothesis itself is necessarily vague, as indeed the Oedipus example shows. The analyst has to give himself room to shift the hypothesis as required to take account of each new version of the myth. Thus when Leach does a Lévi-Strauss experiment with Greek myths and tries to

reconstruct the 'language' to which the Oedipus myth belongs, he comes up with a hypothesis that is only vaguely continuous with the original one. 'Roughly, what it amounts to is simple enough : if society is to go on, daughters must be disloyal to their parents and sons must destroy (replace) their fathers' (Leach 1970, 80). This shifting of the hypothesis is vindicated by Lévi-Strauss in his discussion of another 'version' of Oedipus. 'Our interpretation may take into account the Freudian use of the Oedipus myth and is certainly applicable to it. Although the Freudian problem has ceased to be that of autochthony *versus* bisexual reproduction, it is still the problem of understanding how *one* can be born from *two* : How is it that we do not have only one procreator, but a mother plus a father?' (LS 1958a, 217).

A second feature of the transformational hypothesis which makes it hard to falsify is the descriptive procedure used to apply it, the procedure of characterising the elements in a myth and putting them in columns. There is always some description on the basis of which two units in a myth can be put in the same column because Lévi-Strauss puts no limit on the abstractness of the description; indeed his universalism tends to encourage abstractness. An indefinite number of events could fall under the description 'denial of the autochthonous origin of man'—particularly if Lévi-Strauss's sort of reasoning is accepted as a model. 'The dragon is a chthonian being which has to be killed in order that mankind be born from the Earth; the Sphinx is a monster unwilling to permit men to live ... Since the monsters are overcome by men, we may thus say that the common feature of the third column is *denial of the autochthonous origin of man*' (LS 1958a, 215).

Lévi-Strauss implicitly acknowledges the looseness of his descriptive procedure when he comments in the first volume of *Mythologiques* on the inexhaustibility of mythological analysis. 'There is no real end to mythological analysis, no hidden unity to be grasped once the breaking-down process has been completed. Themes can be split up *ad infinitum*. Just when you think you have disentangled and separated them, you realise that they are knitting together again in response to the operation of unexpected affinities' (LS 1964, 5; see also 17–18, 341). The conclusion he draws in *Mythologiques* is that one analysis is as good as another : the diversity does not worry him because in the end he thinks any analysis will bring him to the one basic structural law. An equally reasonable conclusion might be that if no analysis of any particular myth or at least no restricted set of analyses imposes itself there is something suspect about the analytic method being followed.

The third feature of the transformational hypothesis to affect its falsifiability relates to the concept of transformation itself. The factor relating the different versions of one myth is that they are transformations of the one structure or, as is also said, transformations of one another. The image is a mathematical one. A myth is a transformation of another myth if there is some rule or rules whereby one can pass from the one to the other. Lévi-Strauss extends the image when he says that myths can be transformationally related as symmetrical, inverted, equivalent, and so on. He admits that such relational terms are not precisely defined in his work and hopes that the job of definition can be done later. 'I have used them to refer to large bundles of relations which we vaguely perceive to have something in common' (LS 1964, 31).

If the only constraints put on transformation are that it be achieved by a set of rules then anything can be transformed into anything : you make up the rules as you go along. Thus with a modicum of ingenuity, any two myths could be presented as transformations or versions of one another. The transformational hypothesis does allow something like this to happen. Leach has an interesting comment to make on the hypothesis as he presses it in the case of Greek myths. 'It will be seen that if we proceed in this way there never comes any particular point at which we can say that we have considered "all the variants" for almost any story drawn from the general complex of classical Greek mythology turns out to be a variant in one way or another' (Leach 1970, 79).

There are three types of constraint that can be put on the concept of transformation. The first is that only certain rules or sets of rules should be allowed to count as rules of transformation. Lévi-Strauss may seem to introduce this constraint for he regards inverted, symmetrical, equivalent, and such transformations as the only ones worth considering. He uses these terms in such broad senses however that they put no substantial constraint on the rules of transformation which he is prepared to allow.

The second type of constraint that can be put on transformations is the condition that some content must be preserved over the transformation. This is the constraint that operates in Chomsky's grammar where one sentence is a transform of another only if they have—in some general sense—the same semantic content. There are three such constraints that Lévi-Strauss might want to invoke. The first is that something sensed in the transforms, its resonance or even its meaning, remain the same. He does invoke this when he says in his 1955 paper that 'a myth remains the same as long as it is felt as such' (LS 1958a, 217). This surprisingly intuitive criterion of identity does not reappear in later works. It seems to be out of line with the idea that it is only possible *after* analysis to understand how a native would have experienced a myth. The criterion would offer little assurance of objectivity since the analysis which guided it would be precisely the analysis which claimed to discover a transformational relationship between two myths.

The second content constraint that Lévi-Strauss might want to put on his transformations is that the deep structure of the myths, the underlying opposition, be common to any transforms (see LS 1964, 332; 1971a, 538–9). In one text he says that besides affecting the *armature* of a myth—its set of units—or the code— the way it sets the units off against each other—a transformation may affect the deep structure itself, but here he is using 'deep structure' loosely or he is considering a possibility more extreme than any he meets in his actual analyses (see LS 1971b, 131). The deep structure constraint however is not of much use in restricting what will count as a transformation and what not : this, because Lévi-Strauss is so loose with his hypotheses and so casual about deciding what counts as a single deep structure.

The third content constraint is one which would ensure, not that the same myth is being transformed, but that it is still myth that is in question and not just 'free narrative'. Lévi-Strauss does in fact put such a constraint on those transformations which are to count as transformations between versions of one myth. The constraint amounts to a 'principle of conservation of mythic material' (LS 1971b, 131). Theoretically any number of transformations are possible but only some preserve the mythic quality of myth; only some keep a hidden opposition in play (see LS 1966, 105–6; 1971a, 604). This constraint is hard to apply since it is so difficult—again in view of the vagueness of the transformational hypothesis—to say when there is no longer an opposition presented. In any case it is not the sort of constraint required in the present context.

Apart from the rule constraint and the content constraints the only other type of constraint possible on transformations is that of continuity. This would demand that only those myths which are related by some line of causal or at least cultural continuity should be considered as transformed versions of the same myth. In *Mythologiques* Lévi-Strauss sometimes suggests that a constraint of this type is operative in his treatment of myth—for instance when he explains transformations by the character of different narrators and by the different social circumstances of narration. The suggestion is belied when he insists that from the point of view of his analysis it does not matter whether or not one believes that the myths analysed have a common point of origin in space and time : the belief has no effect on the analysis. He admits that his argument that American myths form a transformational system or set—a 'language'—raises a problem about the development of the myths but denies that it presupposes a solution of the problem. 'I have defined such a set, and I hope that I have supplied proof of its being a set. It is the business of ethnographers, historians, and archaeologists to explain how and why it exists' (LS 1964, 8; see 1971a, 541).

The vague formulation of hypothesis, the description of units in terms of unlimited abstractness, the appeal to transformations in an inadequately constrained sense : these are the faults that I see in Lévi-Strauss's method. They mean that with ingenuity—and this is not something Lévi-Strauss lacks—the analyst of myth can fail to falsify almost any typical hypothesis about the structure underlying a given range of myths. He is allowed to shift the hypothesis to cater for the growing number of versions, vary the level of abstractness of his descriptions to bring all the elements of a version within the required matrix, and invoke any rules of transformation to prove that two myths are really versions of one. With such leeway no analytic goal can seem preposterous.

48.   The goal which Lévi-Strauss sets himself in *Mythologiques* is to show that the myths of South and North America form a system—that they play with the same deep structure and so

carry the same message. The method which he follows is not precisely that of the 1955 paper but an adaptation of it. Less emphasis is now placed on describing each myth and fitting it to a matrix. He is more interested in relating myths transformationally, allowing the structure of each myth to appear in the transformations imposed on it. A new looseness appears here for now there is no single structural description of a myth but a description to suit every transformation : 'themes can be split up *ad infinitum*' (LS 1964, 5). It is only in the last analysis when the full range of myths has been sampled that the underlying opposition which brings the myths together is revealed. Up to then all is flux.

The opposition which Lévi-Strauss claims to find at work in the 813 myths which he considers is a universal cosmological theme. In many of the myths it is not at all clearly present. 'Many hundreds of narratives, very different from each other in appearance and each quite complex on its own account, originate in a series of linked assertions : there is the sky, there is the earth; parity between the two is out of the question; therefore the presence on earth of this heavenly thing, fire, constitutes a mystery. Finally, now that one finds fire here below put to domestic use, the conclusion is inevitable that someone went to the sky to look for it there' (LS 1971a, 539).

The method which yields this conclusion—admittedly an exciting one—is extremely fanciful and shows all the faults analysed in section 47. In these final sections I wish to show how Lévi-Strauss uses it. He begins his analysis with a Bororo myth (henceforth M1) about a boy who rapes his mother, is sent by his father on various deadly missions—the idea being to get rid of him—but comes through thanks to the advice of his grandmother. On the night of his final return to his village a terrible storm extinguishes all fires but his grandmother's—he is staying with her—and the other villagers come the next day to her for embers to relight their own. He is discovered and revealed to his father who behaves civilly towards him. The son has a hunt organised however and during it he changes into a stag and casts his father into a lake where he is devoured by fish. The father's lungs rise to the surface and are the origin of a certain kind of floating leaf.

To get his analysis under way Lévi-Strauss puts this myth side by side with two other Bororo myths which have certain thematic connections with it. The second myth (M2) tells of a boy who sees his mother raped—'incestuously', since by a member of her own moiety—reports this to his father who secretly kills the offending couple, and then sets up a search for his mother—in vain since his father, who has buried her in his tent, misleads him. In the course of the search the boy turns into a bird and drops excrement on his father's shoulder. This grows into a tree and the father leaves the village where he is chief. He discovers that wherever he stops a lake or river springs up—there had been no terrestrial water before—and the tree diminishes; eventually indeed it disappears. Things are very pleasant and he gives up his chiefdom to live in the wild; after a time he is joined by his successor. They return only to bring ornaments, which they make themselves, to the villagers.

The third myth (M3) tells of a boy who refuses to leave his family hut at puberty and go to the men's house. His grandmother tries to poison him with vapours in his sleep but he wakes up and kills her, thrusting an arrow into her anus. The boy's sister cannot find the grandmother to look after her baby when she goes to collect fish that the tribe have poisoned in the lake; she leaves the baby in a tree where it turns into an anteater. At the river the sister stuffs herself with dead fish, suffers horrible pains and breathes out vapours that are the origin of all diseases. Her brothers kill her and throw pieces of her body into the lakes.

Lévi-Strauss argues that there is a common structure in these myths which survives the transformation of particular elements —for instance the transformation in the cause of the hero's wasting away from 'deprivation of a mother who supplied the food' in M2 to 'absorption of antifood (intestinal gas) "supplied" by a grandmother' (LS 1964, 63). The structural core has to do with the fact that in each myth there is an improper conjunction —incest—and then a disjunction which is 'mediated' : for example, in M2 the disjunction of nature and culture is mediated by the ornaments made by the ex-chiefs, in M3 the disjunction of life and death is mediated by the diseases caused by the greedy girl. 'At the start, incest—that is an improper conjunction; at the conclusion, a disjunction that takes place thanks to the appearance of an agent that acts as mediator between the two poles' (LS 1964, 64). This account raises some questions to which

Lévi-Strauss addresses himself. What is the incest in M3? It is symbolic, he says, and consists in the boy's staying in the mother's hut. What is the disjunction which is mediated in M1? This question he uses to lead him further afield.

He goes on to consider six Ge myths about the origin of fire, argues that these are transformations of M1 and that side by side with them M1 reveals the structural aspect under which it mediates a disjunction. The Ge myths tell of a young man who is given refuge by a jaguar with a human wife. The jaguar is friendly and the wife not, and in self-defence the hero kills the wife with weapons provided by the jaguar. He steals fire from the jaguar and brings it back to his tribe, thus providing men with fire for the first time. Put in the context of these myths M1 appears in a new light: it is a myth which explains the origin of wind and rain (anti-fire) and, more weakly, the origin of fire itself. Wind and rain come with the hero's return, fire comes of his grandmother's embers. Fire is the mediating agent in M1. It mediates between heaven and earth, since it comes from heaven to earth; life and death, since it provides food for life; nature and culture, since it makes cooking possible and this transforms the natural into something cultural (see LS 1964, 65).

Lévi-Strauss gives a detailed account of the aspects of the transformation of M1 into the Ge myths; it is worth quoting at length. 'The transformation appears in the following points: (1) a weakening of the polar opposites, in regard to the origin of fire; (2) an inversion of the explicit etiological content, which in this instance is the origin of wind and rain: anti-fire; (3) the mutation of the hero who occupies the position attributed to the jaguar in the Ge myths: master of fire; (4) a correlative inversion of the relations of kinship: the Ge jaguar is the (adopted) father of the hero, whereas the Bororo hero, who is congruous with the jaguar, is a (real) son of a human father; (5) a mutation of family attitudes (equivalent to an inversion): in the Bororo myth the mother is "close" (incestuous), the father "remote" (murderous); in the Ge versions, on the contrary, it is the adopted father who is "close" . . . whereas the adopted mother is "remote", since her intentions are murderous. Lastly, the Bororo hero is not a jaguar (although he discreetly performs the jaguar's function), but we are told that, to kill his father, he turns himself into a deer . . . Several North and South American myths present the jaguar and the deer as a linked and contrasting couple' (LS 1964, 138–9).

49. These examples of Lévi-Strauss's work exemplify his undoubted ingenuity but, equally clearly, the weakness of his method. The method is hardly more than a licence for the free exercise of imagination in establishing associations between myths. The other aspect of the method which is worth illustrating is that which brings Lévi-Strauss out of his particular analyses and transformations towards something ordered, the system in American myths.

Consider the way in which he connects his second volume with the first (see LS 1966, 29–31). In the first we have a system of myths explaining the origin of fire and cooking, S1 (and its inversion, S–1, explaining the origin of water). We also have a system, S2, explaining the origin of meat, something on the 'natural' side of cooking, and its inversion, S–2, explaining the origin of cultural objects—something on the 'cultural' side of cooking. Lévi-Strauss arranges these in the order S–2—S1(S–1) —S2. In the explanation of how meat originated the S2 myths invoked tobacco and so Lévi-Strauss says we should expect a system S3 to the right of S2 which will explain the origin of tobacco; furthermore this system must 'reproduce S1, at least on one axis, so that the group can be considered as closed on that side' (LS 1966, 30). He says that S3 has been considered in the first volume and turns to S–3, a system which he expects to explain the origin of honey, the means invoked by S–2 in explaining the origin of cultural objects. This must reproduce S1 if the group is to be closed on the left side and so reproduce S3 too. Lévi-Strauss begins his second volume with a search for that system. These systems are all strictly sub-systems and provide him with steps on his way to the final system, the one encompassing all American myths.

By its very bulk *Mythologiques* defies summary methodological analysis and criticism but even the examples given indicate that our abstract criticisms in section 47 are borne out in an examination of Lévi-Strauss's actual practice. What method can be put in place of the method he uses? The critical argument developed here would suggest that meaning cannot be put aside and the different 'versions' of a myth boiled down to a single structure.

Structuralist analysis has to explain with reference to a particular text or story how its meaning effects are produced and it must be guided by some intuition of those effects; thus myth analysis must presuppose some understanding of the culture in which the myth arises, some empathy with that culture. To take this view is to join the anthropologist, Mary Douglas, and the classicist, G. S. Kirk (see Douglas 66, Kirk 78). It is to recognise also the irreducible difficulties of myth analysis. No linguistic model, not even a phonological one, can enable the analyst to avoid these.

BIBLIOGRAPHICAL REFERENCES TO III

L. Althusser, *For Marx* (1966), London: Allen Lane, 1969
  Reading Capital (1968) London: New Left Books, 1970
J. A. Boon, *From Symbolism to Structuralism*, Oxford: Blackwell, 1972
M. Douglas, 'The Meaning of Myth' in Leach 1967 (see below)
P. Feyerabend. 'How to be a Good Empiricist' in P. H. Nidditch, ed., *The Philosophy of Science*, Oxford University Press, 1968
M. Foucault, *The Order of Things* (1966), London: Tavistock, 1970
  The Archaeology of Knowledge (1969), London: Tavistock, 1972
H. Gardner, *The Quest for Mind*, New York: Knopf, 1973
M. Glucksmann, *Structuralist Analysis in Contemporary Social Thought*, London: Routledge and Kegan Paul, 1974
E. N. Hayes and T. Hayes, ed., *C. Lévi-Strauss: The Anthropologist as Hero*, Cambridge, Mass.: MIT Press, 1970
R. Jakobson and M. Halle, *Fundamentals of Language*, The Hague: Mouton, 1956
G. S. Kirk, *Myth*, Cambridge University Press, 1970
T. Kuhn, *The Structure of Scientific Revolutions*, London: University of Chicago Press, 2nd edition, 1970
J. Lacan, *Ecrits*, Paris: Seuil, 1966
  Les Quatre Concepts Fondamentaux de la Psychanalyse, Paris: Seuil, 1973
E. Leach, ed., *The Structural Study of Myth and Totemism*, London: Tavistock, 1967
  Genesis as Myth, London: Cape, 1969
  Lévi-Strauss, London: Fontana, 1970
  'Structuralism in Social Anthropology' in Robey—cited above in II
C. Lévi-Strauss, *The Elementary Structures of Kinship* (1949), London: Eyre and Spottiswoode, 1969
  Tristes Tropiques, Paris: Plon, 1955
  Structural Anthropology (1958a), Harmondsworth: Penguin, 1972

'The Story of Asdiwal' (1958b) in Leach (see above) 1967
The Scope of Anthropology (1960), London : Cape, 1967
Totemism (1962a), Harmondsworth : Penguin, 1969
The Savage Mind (1962b), London : Weidenfeld and
    Nicolson, 1966
'Réponses à Quelques Questions', *Esprit*, 1963
The Raw and the Cooked (1964), London : Cape, 1970
From Honey to Ashes (1966), London : Cape, 1973
L'Origine des Manières de Table, Paris : Plon, 1968
L'Homme Nu, Paris : Plon, 1971a
'Comment Meurent les Mythes?' (1971b) in *Science et
    Conscience de la Société, Mélanges en l'honneur de
    Raymond Aron*, Paris, 1971

J. Mepham, 'The Structuralist Sciences and Philosophy' in Robey
—cited above in II

H. G. Nutini, 'Lévi-Strauss's Conception of Science' in Pouillon and
Maranda (see below)

P. Pettit, 'Wittgenstein and the Case for Structuralism', *Journal of
the British Society for Phenomenology* III (1972)

K. Popper, *The Logic of Scientific Discovery*, London : Hutchinson,
1959

J. Pouillon and P. Maranda, ed., *Echanges et Communications,
Mélanges offerts à Claude Lévi-Strauss*, 2 vols., The Hague :
Mouton, 1970

P. Ricoeur, *Freedom and Nature* (1950), Evanston : Northwestern
University Press, 1967
    The Symbolism of Evil (1960), New York : Harper and
    Row, 1967
    Freud and Philosophy (1965), London : Yale University
    Press, 1970

W. G. Runciman, 'What is Structuralism?', *British Journal of
Sociology* XX (1969)

J. P. Sartre, *Being and Nothingness* (1943—cited above in II)
    Critique de la Raison Dialectique, Paris : Gallimard, 1960

Y. Simonis, *Claude Lévi-Strauss ou la 'passion de l'inceste'*, Paris :
Aubier-Montaigne, 1968

R. Young, 'The Historiographic and Ideological Contexts of the
Nineteenth-Century Debate on Man's Place in Nature' in M.
Teich and R. Young, ed., *Changing Perspectives in the History of
Science, Essays in Honour of Joseph Needham*, London : Heine-
mann Educational, 1973

The Value of the Model

50. In this final chapter I intend to discuss the concept of model, with specific reference to semiological inquiry, and develop a perspective from which to review the structuralist use of the linguistic model. My thesis is that the structuralist model is a conceptual framework of the sort often put into operation in science but that science is not what it achieves—at least outside linguistics. The model does not allow the accumulation in a theory of the results of different analyses. What it makes possible —still something of interest—is the formulation of the analyses in homogeneous categories.

To begin the discussion I want to describe a model in general terms as a systematic metaphor. It is a metaphor in the radical sense that it 'carries over' concepts and propositions from one area to another; what is systematic about the metaphor I discuss in section 54 below. The description of a model as a kind of metaphor may seem awkward but that is only because a metaphor consists in a sentence or set of sentences while a model may also mean something extra-linguistic, the reality described by those sentences in their literal usage; the model may have an 'iconic' as well as a 'sentential' sense (see Harré 36). I shall generally use the word, like 'metaphor', in its sentential sense.

The rough definition of metaphor which I take as a starting-point is this : the description of something—the principal subject —in terms that are not normally predicated of it but of something else—the subsidiary subject. The terms in which the metaphor is embodied may serve to classify that of which they are predicated as a certain species of thing or to characterise it by reference to different qualities which it is supposed to possess. Thus the following descriptions are all examples of metaphors.

'Richard is a lion', 'It is a soft day', 'The poor are the negroes of Europe', 'Cambridge is a serene city'.

51. Max Black distinguishes two opposed views of metaphor: the substitution view and the interaction view (Black, chapter 3). By the substitution view the expression on which a metaphor turns—the metaphorical expression—is a substitute for a literal expression, one that applies in the normal way to the principal subject. 'Lion' on this view is simply a replacement for 'brave man'. The view has dominated the theory of metaphor: it suggests the common assessment of it as 'saying one thing and meaning another'. It is a negative view which attributes substantial value to metaphor only in the case where the metaphor replaces an awkward expression and enriches the literal vocabulary. In other cases the substitution view suggests that what was communicated by metaphor could just as well have been communicated in a literal description: the only value of the metaphor is stylistic—it gives some surprise, paints a pretty picture, and so on.

A special form of this view of metaphor is what Black calls the 'comparison view'. This distils 'Richard is a lion' into 'Richard is like a lion—in being brave'; metaphor is reduced to simile. The distinctive feature of the comparison view is that metaphor is still made a replacement for a literal description. Here the basis for the metaphorical description is explicitly provided: the literal expression can be replaced by the metaphorical one because of the similarity indicated between the primary and subsidiary subjects.

The view which Black pits against the substitution view—he adopts it himself—is one he finds in I. A. Richards; he dubs it the 'interaction view'. This grants a specific cognitive or communicative function to metaphor, one that makes most metaphors irreducible to literal descriptions. In interesting metaphors at least—and 'Richard is a lion' is certainly not an example—Richards claims that our thoughts about the two subjects interact to produce a new meaning effect: because of such interaction a metaphor like 'The poor are the negroes of Europe' cannot be paraphrased without remainder.

This account of metaphor is itself metaphorical and Black supplements it with another metaphor: that of a screen or filter.

He maintains that the important thing about a metaphorical expression is not its literal meaning but the system of associations it carries in its literal usage. These associations provide us with a screen through which we view the principal subject in the metaphorical usage of the expression. Take 'Man is a wolf'. This description leads us to see man in terms of those things we associate with wolves which have some resonance in the human situation : their fierceness, their unreliability, their voraciousness, and so on. 'Any human traits that can without undue strain be talked about in "wolf-language" will be rendered prominent, and any that cannot will be pushed into the background. The wolf-metaphor suppresses some details, emphasises others—in short, organises our view of man' (Black 41).

52.   The view of metaphor which I would defend is the interaction view. In this section I want to show that the interaction effect can be explained in terms of the subcategorial rules of grammar invoked by Chomsky (see section 14 above). This will be my only defence of the view.

It is very striking that every transgression of a selectional rule constitutes a potential metaphor, though not always an interesting or attractive one. The metaphor is potential in the sense that it is always possible to imagine a context in which it would have communicative value, being taken precisely as a metaphor. Consider the examples which Chomsky gives of violations of selectional rules :

1.   Colourless green ideas sleep furiously
2.   Golf plays John
3.   The boy may frighten sincerity
4.   Misery loves company
5.   They perform their leisure with diligence (Chomsky 1965, 149—cited above in I).

The nonsense in none of these cases is absolute, as Chomsky himself recognises. In each case a context can be supplied in which the description assumes the status of a metaphor. There are complaints to be made against these metaphors but none of them is that they are nonsense or beyond all interpretation. No. 1 might apply to seeds in spring, though rather unhappily; No. 2, under some strain, to an obsessive golfer; No. 3, humorously, to a devious child; No. 4 to a common sort of situation, with the force of a proverb; No. 5, amusingly if pedantically, to holiday-makers at any seaside.

Consideration of these examples suggests that every transgression of a selectional rule constitutes a potential metaphor. What I want to say is that most metaphors are constituted by such transgressions. (The point is borne out by the examples mentioned in section 50 : the only one of them which does not clearly break a selectional rule is 'The poor are the negroes of Europe', and even this might be debated.) It follows that most metaphors involve a certain sort of nonsense.

It is in fact a very special sort. Selectional rules give expression to what are sometimes called 'restrictions of co-occurrence', restrictions which mark the final and perhaps the weakest boundaries of what can and cannot be said. They define the boundaries, in Gilbert Ryle's sense, of the ontology of types built into a language. 'When a sentence is (not true or false but) nonsensical or absurd, although its vocabulary is conventional and its grammatical construction is regular, we say that it is absurd because at least one ingredient expression in it is not of the right type to be coupled or to be coupled in that way with the other ingredient expression or expressions in it. Such sentences, we may say, commit type-trespasses or break type-rules' (Ryle 1938, 75).

The reason why metaphor can have the interactive power which Black and Richards ascribe to it is precisely that it mixes types which are sacred to literal usage. Good metaphor is constructive nonsense, disrupting the ontology which we grasp in learning the subcategorial or selectional rules of our language. It challenges the way in which we ordinarily see that which it describes and it draws us towards an entirely new perspective on the subject.

53. As I interpret it the interaction view gives primary importance to the disruptive effect of metaphor, its capacity to reorganise our experience. Thus it is necessary to reject a suggestion made—perhaps somewhat lightly—by Cohen and Margalit. 'It is psychogenetically more illuminating to view the literal patterns of word-use as the result of imposing certain restrictions on metaphorical ones, than to view metaphorical patterns as the result of removing certain restrictions from literal ones' (Cohen/

Margalit 723—cited above in I). If there were no selectional restrictions built into language there would be no linguistic organisation of experience. To think of removing those restrictions is to postulate a world in which count objects and mass objects, concrete things and abstract things are of a kind, a world in which water might laugh, ideas dance and tables flow— indiscriminately. The child in such a world could not pick up the organisation of things which is an intrinsic part of linguistic development among us. Nor would he have anything to learn as an adult from metaphor: this could not serve to reorganise experience because there would be nothing for it to reorganise.

Disruption is not enough for good metaphor however: not just any violation of a selectional rule offers a striking reorganisation of our experience. One further element which is certainly necessary is an analogy of some kind between the principal subject and the secondary subject of the metaphor. This analogy makes the two subjects comparable in respect of some property or properties—a man and a wolf in respect of fierceness, unreliability and so on. If we write M for 'man', W for 'wolf' and a, b, c, d, for the properties in respect of which they are comparable the analogy gives us these equations:

$$\frac{M}{a} :: \frac{W}{a} , \frac{M}{b} :: \frac{W}{b} , \text{etc.;}$$

these read, man is to human unreliability in the same way as wolf is to vulpine unreliability, and so on. The analogy relation is reflexive—

$$\frac{M}{a} :: \frac{M}{a} ;$$

symmetrical—if $\frac{M}{a} :: \frac{W}{a}$, then $\frac{W}{a} :: \frac{M}{a}$;

invertible—if $\frac{M}{a} :: \frac{W}{a}$, then $\frac{a}{M} :: \frac{a}{W}$;

and capable of summing to give

$$\frac{M}{a,b,c,d} :: \frac{W}{a,b,c,d}.$$

What distinguishes this sort of analogy from mathematical pro-
portionality is that it is based on a shifting sense of similarity
and not on a rigid formal property. Thus there may be no unique
solution to the problem of a fourth term in an equation of
analogy—the fish's tail corresponds to the bird's tail or to its
wing. Further, the analogy relation is not generally transitive:
it may be true that

$$\frac{\text{fish}}{\text{tail}} :: \frac{\text{bird}}{\text{tail}}$$

and that

$$\frac{\text{bird}}{\text{tail}} :: \frac{\text{girl}}{\text{hair}},$$

but it need not follow that

$$\frac{\text{fish}}{\text{tail}} :: \frac{\text{girl}}{\text{hair}}.$$

(For this account of analogy see Hesse 57–100).

The analogy between two subjects which allows the construction of a good metaphorical description of one or other of them
—it may not be sufficient to guarantee this description—does not
rule out the possibility of a certain disanalogy between the
subjects. On the contrary, such disanalogy seems inevitable.
There will always be some properties in respect of which the two
subjects cannot be sensibly or usefully compared with each other:
the wolf's furriness, man's vulnerability, and so on. There will
also be properties in respect of which it is not clear whether the
subjects are comparable or not; let us call them 'neutral' properties as distinct from analogous or disanalogous ones. They
are important because they make a metaphor open-ended: they

give the metaphor power to suggest questions to which the answers are not obvious and may be interesting.

The disanalogy between the two subjects is one of the reasons why a metaphor, even a common one, may fail to 'die' and so may fail to become part of the literal vocabulary. If the disanalogy is of such a kind that forgetting it would mean putting an important 'boundary' in doubt then any metaphor which it tolerates is likely to remain a metaphor; this at least is a plausible empirical hypothesis. The wolf metaphor and its derivatives are likely to remain metaphors because, even in our urban society, the distinction between the human and the animal—particularly the undomesticated animal—is of some psychological importance; we dare not deny all disanalogy between the two. Catachresis, the fitting of metaphorical expressions into the literal vocabulary, can only work when the disanalogy involves a psychologically unimportant boundary—or a boundary which is too clear to be threatened, and is unimportant in a secondary sense. Black illustrates both cases. 'If a catachresis serves a genuine need, the new sense introduced will quickly become part of the *literal* sense. "Orange" may originally have been applied to the colour by catachresis; but the word is now applied to the colour just as "properly" (and unmetaphorically) as to the fruit. "Osculating" curves do not kiss for long, and quickly revert to a more prosaic mathematical contact. And similarly for other cases' (Black 33).

54. A model is a systematic metaphor. It is systematic in two senses. First, it is a metaphor developed in all the implications that can have bearing on the principal subject. The questions suggested by the neutral properties of the secondary subject are all duly raised. Thus, if we propose taking the narrative text as a 'sentence', a syntagmatically constructed set of paradigmatically defined elements, we are prepared to ask all the questions suggested by the metaphor. What are the elements? What are the different types of syntagmatic constraint? Is there a generative grammar of narrative texts? Is there a descriptive theory to account for such texts? And so on. The linguistic model is no casual analogy for the structuralist but a metaphor which must be pressed systematically for the problems it enables the analyst to formulate.

The second sense in which the metaphor is systematic is not so obvious. The use of a metaphor may be preceded by discussion of the subsidiary subject, which has the effect of controlling the associations carried over in the metaphor. 'An author can do much to suppress unwanted implications of the word "contract", by explicit discussion of its intended meaning, before he proceeds to develop a contract theory of sovereignty' (Black 43). This discussion makes a metaphor systematic in another sense : it frees it from the caprice of every day imagination in assigning associations to the secondary subject. Structuralism makes its metaphor systematic in this sense when it draws on a specific tradition of linguistics for its understanding of language. That linguistics systematically controls the associations carried over to non-linguistic semiological objects when they are described in linguistic terms; it determines the questions which the metaphor is meant to suggest. Thus the text becomes not just a 'sentence' but, precisely, 'a syntagmatically constructed set of paradigmatically defined elements'.

55.   In section 21 we distinguished between two kinds of model, the homeomorph and the paramorph. Properly speaking, it is only the paramorph which is a model, a systematic metaphor. The homeomorph—the linguistic model when it is used to provide a model of stylistic devices—is constructed by abstraction from the phenomena of language itself and by idealisation of them. The Saussurian description of language does sometimes invoke the metaphor of a mechanism but not in any systematic way : the metaphor serves to underline the novelty of the description, its break with the speaker's immediate experience of language. It is only the paramorph—the linguistic model when it is used to describe the literary, non-literary and customary arts —that is intrinsically metaphorical. Here the subsidiary subject, language, is quite distinct from the principal subjects for which it provides the model. Here we have the systematic carry-over of concepts and propositions from one area to another.

Once a model—by this I shall mean a paramorphic model—is seen as a systematic metaphor, its role in inquiry becomes visible. That role may be a more important one than has been traditionally recognised. Take what R. B. Braithwaite says about using models : 'to do this avoids the complications and difficulties involved in having to think explicitly about the language or other form of symbolism by which the theory is represented' (Braithwaite 92). He takes a view of the model in science which corresponds to the substitution view of metaphor. The model is seen as a dispensable convenience or decoration which stands in for the literal descriptions of formal theory. This indeed is what a model may be but our discussion of metaphor shows that it may also be something very much more important. It may be an epistemologically crucial means of reorganising the way the scientist looks at certain phenomena and theorises about them. I believe that this is what it generally is.

The view of the model which I am proposing has been defended in recent years by a small number of scientists and philosophers: for example, Max Black, Rom Harré, Mary Hesse and E. H. Hutten (see Bibliographical References below; also *Cambridge Review*). Harré presents the view in particularly dramatic terms: '*The Copernican Revolution in the Philosophy of Science* is to see the traditional view that a deductive system of laws is the heart of a theory, and an associated picture of the mechanisms and permanent objects ... but a heuristic device, turned upside down. It is to see the model as essential and the achievement of a deductive system among the laws as a desirable heuristic device' (Harré 2).

To extend the interaction view from the metaphor to the model is to see that the structuralist use of the linguistic model is, potentially at least, of some importance. We are not dealing with a bizarre piece of French nonsense—at least not necessarily. The introduction of the linguistic model is the kind of thing we should expect of a new departure in scientific inquiry. Whether or not it is successful, structuralism certainly offers a proper sort of strategy for semiological investigation.

56.   There are models and models however, metaphors and metaphors. We have spoken as if models in science—and the theories which spell them out—are all at the same explanatory level vis-à-vis the facts. This is misleading. One of the things that has become clear in recent philosophy of science is that the scientist is theoretically committed at different levels. In order to consider the respective claims of two theories at a first level he must assume at a second level the validity of the theoretical out-

look that makes those seem the only alternatives. At the highest level some historians claim to see in the development of natural science a movement, presupposed by more particular movements, from one metaphysical theory to another. 'Since its beginnings in antiquity scientific knowledge has been articulated under one of three main metaphysical systems, which have served to provide, for each epoch, the forms of explanation. The three systems under which scientific mankind has so far lived are the Aristotelian system, the Corpuscularian philosophy, and the theory of the Plenum. They pictured the world respectively as Matter differentiated by Forms, as Moving Atoms in the Void, as a Universal Field in various and changing States of Strain' (Harré 124—cited above in II).

At what level does the linguistic model operate in directing semiological inquiry? What sort of theory does it provide, metaphysical or scientific, conceptual or empirical? I suggested in section 2 and have assumed throughout that it provides a metaphysical or conceptual theory. I must now present my view in detail and allow the case for it to appear clearly. I take metaphysical theory in the sense of categorial or conceptual framework and I follow in general Stefan Körner's analysis of what such a framework involves (see Körner).

In the language of metaphor, what I think structuralism provides or tries to provide with the linguistic model is an 'archetype' or governing metaphor for semiological inquiry. Black claims to find such a metaphor at work in Kurt Lewin's sociological field theory. 'We repeatedly encounter such words as "field", "vector", "phase-space", "tension", "force", "boundary", "fluidity"—visible symptoms of a massive archetype awaiting to be reconstructed by a sufficiently patient critic' (Black 241). What I hope to give in the account of the structuralist conceptual framework is a reconstruction of precisely such a massive archetype.

57. To categorise or conceptualise any region of reality—or indeed reality as a whole, if such is one's ambition—is to make a division first of all between particulars and attributes; then a second division between the dependent and independent entities in each group; finally a third division within each of the four sub-groups between what Körner calls maximal kinds or cate-

gories. This at least is the full procedure: one may discount any one of the divisions as irrelevant for one's purposes.

The first division is a much controverted distinction, drawn on grounds of logic (see Strawson, Part 2; also Dummett, chapters 7 and 14, and Searle, chapters 4 and 5—both cited above in I). I will take particulars as things which are naturally denoted by expressions other than the nominalisations of predicates, attributes as things which are not naturally denoted in this way. Thus 'the man' or 'John' denotes a particular, 'wisdom' or 'being wise'—nominalisations of 'is wise'—an attribute.

The second division is a distinctively ontological one. A dependent particular is one which can only exist so long as something else exists; similarly for a dependent attribute. Unless one is a platonist one will want to say that all attributes are dependent, needing particulars in which to 'inhere'. Unless one is a holist one will want to say that many particulars are independent; and unless one is an atomist one will want to say that many also are dependent.

The third division is usually drawn for a specific area, on specific grounds. If it is drawn for the whole of reality the grounds may well be supplied by the restrictions of co-occurrence on different terms.

The divisions are represented in the diagram on the following page.

Our interest is in the categorisation given by the linguistic model for any area to which it is applied. It will focus on the different categories of particular and attribute distinguished by the model. For each of these categories we must, according to Körner, find a constitutive attribute which says what something must be to belong to the category, and an individuating attribute which says what it must be to be a distinct individual.

58.   The linguistic model allows three basic kinds of particular: the elements which correspond to words, the strings which correspond to sentences and the systems which correspond to languages. Each of these entities is provided with a constitutive and an individuating attribute. Take the element first. This is constituted by being paradigmatically and syntagmatically—say, ps- —related to other elements. It is individuated by how it is ps-related to what, on the principle of indiscernibles: two

Figure 2

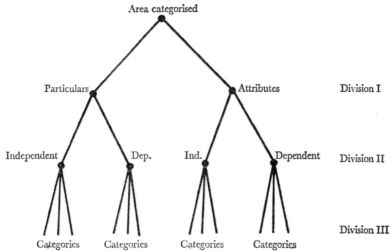

elements with precisely the same ps-relations are, for the purposes of the framework, one and the same element.

The string in the structuralist framework is constituted by being articulated out of elements in accordance with the ps-relations of those elements; equivalently, it is constituted by being generated by a system. The string is individuated on the other hand by what elements are articulated in it, and how—in what order; again the principle of indiscernibles applies.

It may be worth remarking here that both of the principles of individuation introduced have certain unusual results. The principle individuating elements would make perfect synonyms indistinguishable. This is because it does not take into account the individuation of elements prior to their absorption into the system under discussion : in the case of words, their individuation within a phonological system as discrete sound combinations.

The principle individuating strings has the equally unusual result that it refuses the title of 'same sentence' to sentences which have the same meaning, and even perhaps the same words; all that need differ to mark them as different sentences is the word order. This happens because the framework does not allow a principle of individuation deriving from the function served by strings—in this case communication. What it does admit that leaves room for a more liberal sense of individuation is transformability. This is a corollary attribute to being articulated or being generated and means that any string can be transformed, in a limited number of steps, into any other string. When the transformation can be done in very few steps, perhaps without the replacement of any elements, and especially when something is preserved over the transformation, then it is plausible to extend one's sense of individuation and speak of the transforms as forms of the one string. Thus two sentences become the expressions of the same proposition, two musical sequences variations on the same theme, two narratives versions of the one story.

The third kind of semiological particular is the system. It is constituted through ps-relating elements with one another or, equivalently, through generating strings; this is what the ps-relating of elements makes possible. The system is individuated by what precisely it ps-relates and how; again, the principle of indiscernibles is all that need be invoked.

The categorisation of particulars forces a corresponding categorisation of attributes. The constitutive attributes we have introduced are : ps-related, articulated (generated, transformable) and ps-relating (generating). We need not define an attribute to constitute any one of these in turn but may take them all as basic; in this way we avoid regress. We find a problem with their individuation. The attributes each define a class—whether of elements, strings or systems—and each may seem to be individuated by what elements are in its class (see Quine 209). This individuation however is inadequate because it makes a single attribute of 'articulated', 'generated' and 'transformable', which define the same class; similarly with 'ps-relating' and 'generating'. All we can say perhaps is that attributes are individuated on an intuitive basis.

It is now possible to represent in a diagram the conceptual framework which structuralists get from the linguistic model : see Figure 3. This account of the structuralist conceptual framework is not the only account that might be given of it. Parts might be changed around : for instance if relations were taken as particulars. And parts might be added : for instance if the attributes were broken down into more specific attributes. The account offered is an attempt to show, in fairly rough terms, what the framework looks like; it is not meant as a final statement.

Figure 3

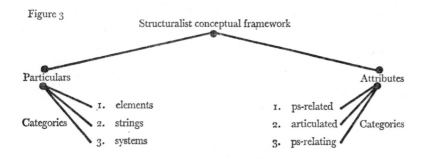

59. It should now be clear that what structuralism derives from the linguistic model is primarily a metaphysic. This metaphysic tells the analyst what sort of thing a semiological object like language is and what sorts of things it involves. Edmund Leach has made the point already: 'structuralism is neither a theory nor a method but "a way of looking at things"' (Leach 1973, 37—cited above in III). This way of looking at things reveals in semiological objects something much better defined and something much more interesting than our everyday concepts allow us to see there. It constructs a reality that looks as if it can bear systematic inquiry.

The idea of any metaphysic in science, any conceptual framework, is that it should allow questions to be asked which are such that the answers to them can assume theoretical form and be assimilated within a system of laws. The structuralist framework certainly allows questions to be asked which look more interesting than the questions that everyday concepts might suggest. The model which it fits to semiological objects has enough neutral properties to release a range of systematically ordered problems; without a model the only questions possible would be casual queries incapable of directing a systematic inquiry.

The disappointing thing about the structuralist framework is that the answers to its questions do not seem capable of being assumed within a theory in any area outside language itself.

There are two lines of questioning along which theory seems a prospect : one would lead to generative theory, the other to descriptive. Neither of these lines is open and the structuralist is left with those questions which are only capable of producing analyses of particular strings or sets of strings. What either theory would have given him—so the framework suggests—is an account of the system presupposed in any area by such strings. The analysis for which he must settle offers no view of that system but concentrates, more or less systematically, on the particular devices that particular strings put into operation. Unlike theory the analysis does not give a general comparative perspective on the strings generated by any system; it offers explanations but not abstractly derivable ones.

The line of inquiry that would lead to generative theory is closed because in no semiological area outside language do we have a firm intuitive sense of what is a well-formed string and what is not. Without such a syntagmatic sense it is impossible to think of working out a system of rules which would 'recognise' the well-formed string and assign it a structure. This argument has already been presented in some detail (see section 24 above).

The argument against descriptive theory has not been developed to the same extent. It can be put in the form of a dilemma which confronts the structuralist who would pursue this theory in any semiological area. He must define the elements with which he is concerned in abstract terms—roughly speaking —or in concrete ones. In the second case he will be led straight to the discussion of particular strings and what was to be general theory will quickly become particular analysis—probably of a systematic kind. In the first case he will be better able to keep his distance from particular strings and to work out the abstract possibilities of combination among his chosen elements. What happens here however is that the abstractly defined combinations do not link up sufficiently tightly with the particular strings which we want to illuminate : usually, any combination will be capable of being associated with a number of significantly different strings. Thus the general theory will be of little semiological interest, it will not serve the primary goal of explaining how different strings produce distinctive meanings.

When it is pressed, the critique of the abstract descriptive theory converges on the critique of the generative theory. The structuralist will argue that it may be possible to find terms of just the 'right' abstraction to define the elements of a descriptive theory. This theory would be able to show the abstract possibilities of combination among the elements and would also be able to link up particular combinations uniquely with particular strings. The nearest thing to such a theory in the literature is Barthes's theory in *Système de la Mode*; this is an abstract combinatory scheme which generates outfits with fairly specific definition (see section 33 above). Here also the abstract combinations fail to link up with the particular strings but for a very interesting reason.

The proper link-up would mean that the significant differences between particular strings would be reflected in the theoretically derivable differences between their abstract correlates. The significant differences are those that mark subtle variations in syntagmatic propriety : the differences that make this outfit 'just right', the other 'that fraction vulgar'. These differences would be theoretically reflected if the theory could define syntagmatic laws expressing such subtle restrictions of combination. Such laws are impossible for the same reason that generative rules are impossible. Our intuitive sense of the well-formed string is not firm enough outside language to guide the formulation of such laws; our perception of structure is too little the result of a deduction, too much the outcome of a fickle sense of the *gestalt*. It is not surprising that what Barthes offers is a theory of the physically possible combinations within his outfit scheme, not a theory showing the fashionably possible ones. His theory like any abstract descriptive theory fails to link up in an interesting way with particular strings.

60.   There are few complications about straight semiological analysis. Here the analyst takes the structuralist conceptual framework and tackles straightaway the questions which it suggests should be put to any particular string or set of strings. What is the structure by reference to which this string can be understood? What are the elements which work within the structure to produce the meaning of the string? What particular contrasts give each element its particular significance? And so on.

Systematic analysis is more complicated, and more interesting. Here the analyst introduces a set of categories—I will say, an analytic schema—which knits the conceptual framework more tightly to the particular sort of string under analysis. The schema specifies the framework in the sense that it specifies the questions suggested by the framework so that they are better suited to the analysis on hand. Thus Barthes's scheme in S/Z puts aside general questions about structure, elements and contrasts in favour of specific questions about the different semiological roles which pieces of text play: these roles may be 'proairetic' for example, 'hermeneutic' or 'semic' (see section 26 above).

The analytic schema corresponds to the specific theory in scientific inquiry. The difference between the schema and the theory is that the schema does not accumulate in any significant way the results of the analyses which it directs. The generative or descriptive theory would direct analyses too but the results of the analyses would be fed back into the theory: they would suggest, strengthen or illustrate propositions derivable within the theory—its axioms and theorems. The analytic schema does not have this capacity to recover the results of analyses, give them theoretical form and hold them constant from analysis to analysis. The analysis that it directs of a semiological string is never a replication, it is always something unique.

What I am saying is that there is an art of semiological analysis —in the literary, the non-literary and the customary areas— never, in a strict sense, a science; the key word is 'skill', not 'method'. Robert Scholes has this to say about literary criticism. 'Our discipline is a science to the extent that it is cumulative and an art to the extent that each critical work is unique' (Scholes 77—cited above in II). I believe that like the other disciplines which interest structuralism it will remain always an art.

61.   To reduce the aspirations of structuralism to analysis is not to make little of the movement. The model which structuralism introduces, the framework by which it categorises the areas for semiological analysis, is an important contribution. Negatively, it enables us to see just why it is not possible to have semiological science: this is a hard lesson but for that very reason one which needs proclaiming. More positively, the structuralist conceptual framework sets the scene well for semiological analysis, it constructs objects fit for systematic investigation.

In some cases the framework has stimulated that investigation, in others it serves to interpret work already done. In most of the cases where it serves an interpretative purpose there is already an analytic schema available. In the non-literary arts there is the *gestalt* schema for describing music, architecture and painting, and in the customary there is the schema provided by the stage metaphor for describing presentation. These schemas can be regarded as analytic schemas which specify the structuralist conceptual framework. The value of seeing them in this way is that it brings together disciplines which seem unrelated but do in. fact have significant affinities. It must be admitted however that these analytic schemas are detachable from the structuralist framework; they can work without it. Even where it is valid and helpful the framework is not always indispensable.

A last objection which may be made against the structuralism we have salvaged is that semiological analysis is uninteresting in any case; the only worthwhile goal for inquiry is theoretical and scientific. This is to make the negative lesson of structuralism a cause for total disillusion. The objection is rooted in a deep assumption of the scientific age that inquiry is for theory or for nothing. What is needed to combat this assumption is a critical philosophy of science of the sort proposed by Jürgen Habermas (see Habermas, 301–17). Man's understanding of how he produces constructions in meaning may be of necessity different from his understanding of how natural or even social systems work having a different constitutive interest. This is the possibility which the philosophy of science must consider in the wake of the structuralist experience. We must learn to forget the positivist dream which Lévi-Strauss dreamed for semiology : 'if it resigns itself to a period in purgatory beside the social sciences, it is because it does not despair of awakening among the natural sciences when the last trumpet sounds' (Lévi-Strauss 1960, 31— cited above in III). Wherever semiology awakens it will not be among the natural sciences.

BIBLIOGRAPHICAL REFERENCES TO IV

M. Black, *Models and Metaphors*, Ithaca, N.Y. : Cornell University Press, 1962

R. B. Braithwaite, *Scientific Explanation*, Cambridge University Press, 1953

Cambridge Review vol. 95, no. 2218 (February 1974) : 'The Scientific Imagination'

J. Habermas, *Knowledge and Human Interests*, London : Heinemann Educational, 1972

R. Harré, *The Principles of Scientific Thinking*, London : Macmillan, 1970

M. Hesse, *Models and Analogies in Science*, Notre Dame, Indiana : University of Notre Dame Press, 1966

E. H. Hutten, *The Ideas of Physics*, Edinburgh : Oliver and Boyd, 1967

S. Körner, *Categorial Frameworks*, Oxford : Blackwell, 1970

W. V. O. Quine, *Word and Object*, Cambridge, Mass. : MIT Press, paperback, 1964

G. Ryle, 'Categories', *Proceedings of the Aristotelian Society* XXXVIII (1938)

P. F. Strawson, *Individuals*, London : Methuen, 1959